The Road Ahead

GW01418799

THE
ROAD
AHEAD

A Self-help Guide for Road Trauma Sufferers and Their Carers

ALEX BLASZCZYNSKI, Dip Psych, PhD, MAPsS

PAULA PANASETIS, BSc Psych (Hons)

DERRICK SILOVE, MD, FRANZCP

Psychiatry Research and Teaching Unit, School of Psychiatry, University of New South Wales, and South Western Sydney Area Health Service, Liverpool Hospital, Liverpool, NSW

A Motor Accidents Authority of New South Wales funded project

UNSW PRESS

A UNSW Press book

Published by
University of New South Wales Press Ltd
University of New South Wales
Sydney 2052 Australia

©Alex Blaszczynski, Paula Panasetis & Derrick Silove 1998

First published in 1998

This book is copyright. Apart from any fair dealing for the purpose of private study, research, criticism or review, as permitted under the Copyright Act, no part may be reproduced by any process without written permission. Inquiries should be addressed to the publisher.

National Library of Australia
Cataloguing-in-Publication entry:

Blaszczynski, Alex, 1949– .
The road ahead: a self-help guide for road trauma sufferers and their carers.

Includes bibliography and index.
ISBN 0 86840 688 0.

1. Traffic accidents—Australia—Psychological aspects. 2. Post-traumatic stress disorder—Treatment. 3. Traffic accident victims—Australia—Rehabilitation. I. Panasetis, Paula. II. Silove, Derrick, 1951– . III. Title.

617.10280994

Design by *Dana Lundmark*
Printed by *South China Printing, Hong Kong*

CONTENTS

ACKNOWLEDGMENTS

The type of work we have been engaged in cannot be carried out without important contribution from many people with diverse abilities. In particular, we wish to express our deep gratitude to Professor Ken Hillman and Dr David Sloane for their active support and encouragement, and in seeing the clinical value of our work and influencing others to do the same.

We would like to acknowledge the financial assistance of the Motor Accidents Authority of New South Wales for providing much needed research funds. Without this support it would not have been possible to develop this book.

We would also like to thank the many people who helped in the preparation of this book. Special thanks goes to Ms Tam Isaacs, project officer, who conducted literature and resource searches and collated relevant material for the original treatment manual used in the patient groups. Her pilot-testing of book chapters and recommended technique with patient groups provided us with a strong basis from which to expand and develop our ideas and helped shape the present self-help book.

We are indebted to many of our colleagues, in particular Beverley Lanesman and Vijaya Manicavasagar who have provided valuable guidance and practical help in the early development of this book. Tony Homer provided helpful discussions and useful comments. Our appreciation is extended to him and to other staff members: Sue Cremer for her critical reviews, Nediljka Dusevic for her suggestion of the title, and Kylie Gordon for her assistance in the initial assessment of the clientele for our group program. We gratefully acknowledge Rod and Gaven Isaacs for their support and critical readings of parts of the book. Our thanks also go to Thelma King who gave generously of her time and secretarial skills in proofreading and editing portions of the book.

We are greatly indebted to Pat Igoe, Co-ordinator of the Road Trauma Support Team Inc (Tasmania), and Dr Richard Bryant, Lecturer and Co-ordinator of the Clinical Psychology Masters Program, School of Psychology, UNSW, for their insightful comments and suggestions in improving the final version of this book.

Finally, we would like to express our heartfelt gratitude to the survivors of road trauma who participated in our program and who shaped our understanding of road trauma reactions.

Without the interest and support of all those mentioned, the task would have been much more difficult and the results certainly less satisfying. Our warmest thanks to all.

Alex Blaszczynski
Paula Panasetis
Derrick Silove

ABOUT THIS GUIDE

PURPOSE OF THIS SELF-HELP GUIDE

Traumatic events can affect the person directly involved, their family, accident witnesses and emergency workers. Accidents can upset an individual's sense of well-being, confidence, self-esteem and security, leading to much distress. Considerable interest and attention has been paid to the effects of dramatic natural disasters such as earthquakes, bushfires, floods and cyclones, as well as tragedies of war, torture and major accidents. But there is also an increasing recognition that motor vehicle accidents are capable of producing similar severe traumatic responses. Traumatic reactions may occur even if the injury sustained is minor.

Many people become confused and anxious about the changes in behaviour and emotions that follow a road trauma. In this guide the terms 'road trauma' and 'motor vehicle accident' are used interchangeably and apply to any accident involving a motor vehicle, motor cycle, truck or bus, and in which the injury may be sustained by drivers, riders, passengers and/or pedestrians. Traumatic reactions may also be experienced by witnesses of the accident and attending emergency workers.

The purpose of this self-help book is to educate road trauma survivors about the types of emotional and psychological reactions that are commonly experienced after road trauma and the importance of seeking professional assistance when these reactions persist. Gaining an understanding of such processes is the first step in learning how you can prevent or minimise emotional symptoms or, in its most severe form, a Post-Traumatic Stress Disorder (PTSD). This is a condition that some people develop after they have experienced an upsetting traumatic event or events, and it is vital to seek professional assistance. Consult your local community health centre or general practitioner for further advice.

The objectives of this book are:

1 **To provide you with information and an understanding of the problems that you may have following an accident. These may affect: *physical, emotional, cognitive* and *behavioural* functioning.**

2 **To assist your family, friends and relatives to better understand what is happening to you. They are also affected by the accident, and the information in this book will help them to provide support and encouragement.**

3 **To increase your skills so that you can cope with symptoms of trauma. This is done by providing you with a range of techniques to deal with your thoughts, feelings and behaviours.**

4 **To alert you to the importance of seeking professional assistance when it becomes too difficult to cope on your own. Asking for help is not a sign of weakness. There are various services which are especially dedicated to helping people who have gone through a traumatic experience. Please do not hesitate to seek further help from your local health professional at any stage.**

Remember

This book aims to reassure you that:

- **Any traumatic reactions you experience are understandable.**
- **You are not the only person to suffer such reactions.**
- **You are not going crazy.**
- **You are not losing control.**

There are many common reactions or symptoms following trauma, such as:

- **loss**
- **anger**
- **numbness**
- **intense fear**
- **confusion**
- **and many others.**

These symptoms are frequently seen and are to be expected as the body and mind try to recover from the shock of an accident. Even though these reactions are common it is often very helpful to discuss them with a professional clinician when they occur so as to determine whether more expert assistance is required.

HOW TO USE THIS GUIDE

This book is designed to provide those affected by road trauma with an understanding of the emotional and psychological reactions that are commonly experienced. This book is not meant to be used as a substitute for professional treatment and may not be suitable for people who are suffering from more severe and multiple reactions and those who have sustained brain injury. Professional assistance should be sought in these cases.

This book is organised in a step-by-step format. It contains practical tasks to complete each week, which are designed to help you practise and apply the principles discussed in each section. Remember, the more consistent the effort, the more positive the result. To obtain lasting improvement you must be prepared to practise the skills as often as possible. Do not become complacent. You will achieve goals only if you are actively doing things, not by merely reading about what has to be done.

It is very important that you understand that the more you do yourself, the more benefit you will receive.

To gain maximum benefit:

- **Read through all sections.**
- **Do the set practical exercises.**
- **Do the relaxation exercises regularly.**
- **Explain the program to those close to you.**
- **Start looking for things you can do and ways of doing them.**
- **Seek professional assistance if in doubt.**

It is important for you to realise that coping is a skill that has to be learnt and practised.

You will learn skills that will enable you to cope with your problems, however it will require time and effort to learn these skills.

This guide can also to be used as a means to monitor and record your progress. Monitoring your progress means writing down things that happen to you, how you react, and what action you have taken. This is very important. It will provide you with the opportunity to collect information about how you have tackled situations effectively, and may also help in future situations.

Be aware

Setbacks *do* occur sometimes during the course of recovery, even for people making excellent progress. However, it is important to keep in mind that no matter how badly you feel during a setback it is very rare for you to go back to the level of distress experienced after the accident.

Although it would be great if the pattern of recovery resembled the pattern shown in Figure 1, this is rarely the case.

In most cases the pattern of recovery is something like the pattern-shown in Figure 2.

Although the occasional setbacks do occur, the more you practice the coping techniques, the smaller the setbacks and the quicker your recovery will be. Remember, even though setbacks occur, the overall progress continues to improve over the longer term.

If you find that your symptoms and reactions are persisting and are becoming worse, it is advisable to seek professional assistance as soon as possible. Consult your local general practitioner or community health centre for more information on available services.

Figure 1
Ideal pattern of
steady recovery
over time

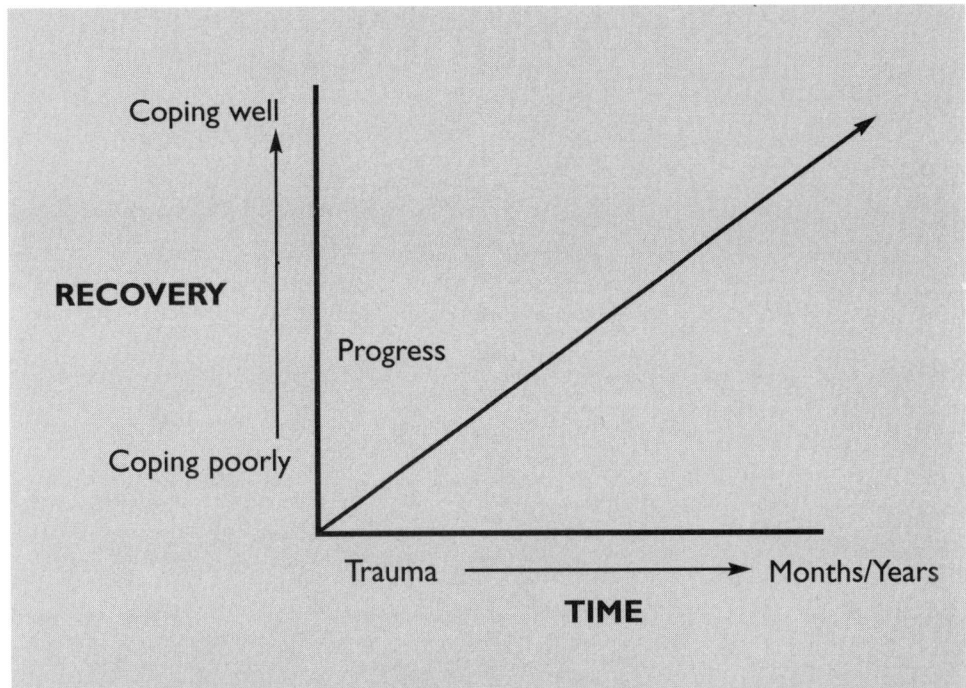

Figure 2
Realistic pattern of
recovery over time

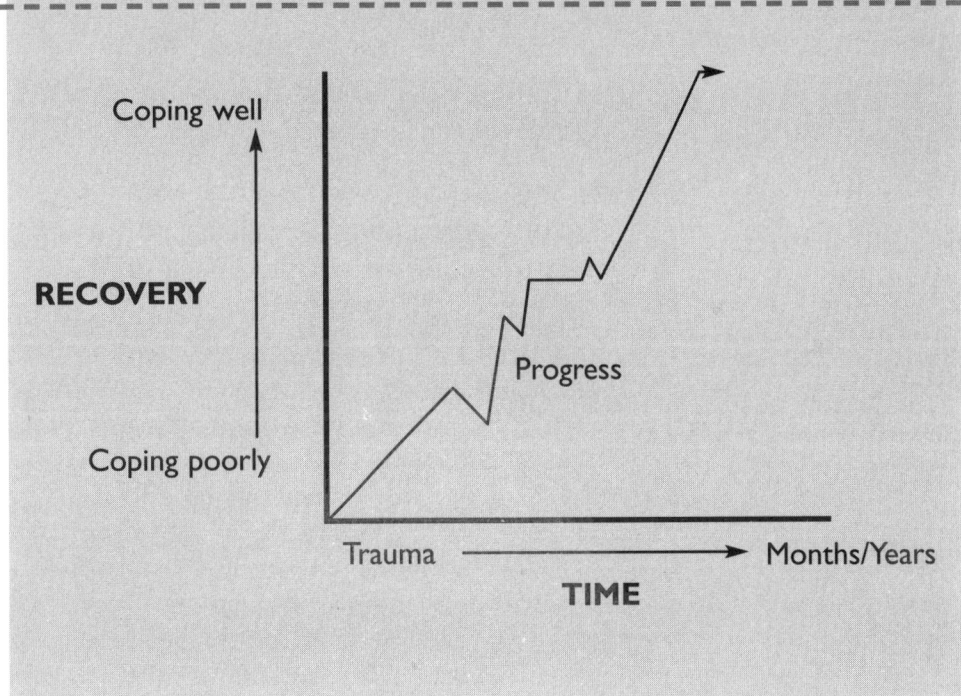

1 INTRODUCTION

Peter N

Peter, a 35-year-old bricklayer, was driving his ute to work early one morning. It was cold and difficult to see in the thick fog so he slowed down to about 40 kilometres per hour and switched on his high beam. He decided he would stop and wait for the fog to lift and also check his street directory for an alternate route. Just as he was about to turn off into a side street however, one of his tyres blew sending the ute over to the other side of the road and in the path of an oncoming truck. He didn't remember much of what happened afterwards but when he woke up in hospital he was told that he was lucky to be alive. He had a broken collar bone, two broken ribs, a broken wrist, a fractured pelvis, broken left tibia, cuts and bruises.

He was allowed to go home after one month as he began showing a good and steady recovery. He was told that he would not be able to work for at least five months. This was very distressing for Peter who was the sole provider for the family and whose wife was pregnant with their fourth child. He started to worry excessively about money, the mortgage, the children and whether he would ever be able to work as a bricklayer again. He lost his appetite, was not sleeping very well and began to lose interest in all usual activities. He constantly complained about his lack of energy and fatigue and was very irritable when around people. He became distant and found it very difficult to show any affection towards his wife and children.

WHAT IS THERE TO KNOW ABOUT MOTOR VEHICLE ACCIDENTS?

Motor vehicle accidents are a common occurrence. In 1996 there were 21 876 people hospitalised as a result of road crashes across Australia. A further 1970 people were killed.[1] These figures do not include the thousands of accidents where people did not require hospitalisation.

If we understand what is happening to ourselves it is less likely that we will panic.

Unfortunately, accidents may cause trauma or emotional shock, especially if severe injuries, threat to life or exposure to distressing scenes occur. Accidents may impact not only on drivers, passengers or pedestrians but also on witnesses, emergency workers and on the family and relatives of survivors.

When people are injured in an accident it is necessary to treat their physical injuries and to provide rehabilitation services necessary for full recovery. Unfortunately, any psychological impact caused by the injury or accident may be often overlooked during normal medical treatment. Not being aware of the psychological impact, especially over the long term, may lead to ongoing distress for the accident survivors, their families and their friends. This emotional trauma disrupts the belief that we can control our bodies and our immediate surroundings, leaving us feeling vulnerable, helpless and unsure of our future.

- - - - - - - -
Remember

Although you may feel alone in your distress, it is important to be aware that your family, relatives and friends are also affected by your distress following the accident. They do care.

WHAT IS A TRAUMA?

A trauma is a sudden unexpected distressing event. Traumas may be due to natural disasters (floods, earthquakes, large fires) or manmade ones (motor vehicle accidents, robberies, physical assaults, industrial accidents). However, whatever type of disaster you have experienced, it is common to experience a range of thoughts, feelings and behaviours that include shock, disbelief, anger, numbness, intense fear, confusion or trembling. These symptoms, which will be described in detail later, can occur quite soon after an accident or may develop at a later stage.

Symptoms may occur in isolation or cluster together in a typical pattern. If they occur within one month then the syndrome is called 'Acute Stress Disorder'. If the symptoms take longer to occur and last for some time, then this is referred to as 'Post-Traumatic Stress Disorder' (PTSD).

Unfortunately, motor vehicle accident injuries, even those of a non-serious nature, may lead to PTSD. The proportion of people who develop PTSD ranges from almost zero[2] to 65–100 percent,[3,4] although more recent research is showing that the more reliable figure is around 20 percent.

It is vital, therefore, to understand that the symptoms of PTSD are signs that our bodies are recovering from a severe stress and do not mean that the sufferer is 'going crazy' or completely losing control. Nevertheless, professional assistance should be sought in order to lessen the intensity and duration of such symptoms.

WHAT HAPPENS AFTER A MOTOR VEHICLE ACCIDENT?

The emotional shock we experience following an accident may cause a stress reaction which can then affect our mood and enjoyment in life. We often have unrealistic expectations of ourselves following a traumatic situation. We believe we 'should cope' or that we 'should be better sooner'. It is important to realise that anyone can develop a stress reaction following road trauma, even people who believed themselves to have been previously strong and stable. Reacting this way does not suggest that we have a weak personality or coping style. It is important that we give ourselves permission to feel 'bad' or 'down' or to cry if we feel the need. Seeking professional assistance should also not be regarded as a sign of weakness. Health professionals are especially trained to help people manage and overcome these types of difficulties.

Mary A

Mary was a 25-year-old single secretary who was travelling to work with her younger sister. As they proceeded to drive through an intersection, a vehicle approaching from their left failed to stop and collided with Mary's car, hitting the front passenger door. The impact forced Mary's car to roll, finally coming to rest on the driver's side.

Mary looked up to see her sister lying motionless, and fluid flowing on the road near the window of her door. Two distressing thoughts came to mind: that her sister was dead, and that the fluid was petrol about to ignite and burn her to death.

Fortunately, neither Mary nor her sister sustained major injuries. Both were bruised and suffered lacerations to the face, arms and legs. Although Mary recovered well physically, she experienced considerable tension, discomfort and fear. She experienced fear whenever she travelled in a car, was unable to drive within a kilometre of the accident scene and suffered recurring panic attacks. She felt guilt for exposing her sister to a life-threatening situation and intense anger towards the driver of the other vehicle.

She became preoccupied with thoughts of death and recurring images of her sister lying motionless and the vehicle bursting into flames. She became depressed, cried often and was unable to concentrate. As a result she was unable to work. Her self-esteem fell and she became socially withdrawn and reluctant to leave home.

As can be seen from the above example there are many issues that may need attention when trying to help someone overcome the effects of an accident.

These issues can be grouped into two categories:

- *Physical*: **injuries sustained.**
- *Psychological*: **emotional distress.**

PHYSICAL INJURIES

Physical injuries still occur at an alarming rate despite new standards in car designs, improved manufacturing techniques and legislation, that is, mandatory seat belt and random breath testing.

The most common injuries people suffer include:

- **bruising (across the chest and abdomen from seat belts)**
- **lacerations**
- **fractures**
- **head injuries**
- **spinal injuries**
- **whiplash**
- **loss of limbs.**

Some people may recover from motor vehicle accident injuries relatively quickly with few lasting physical problems. In other instances prolonged periods of hospitalisation are followed by intense periods of physical rehabilitation.

Seemingly minor injuries such as whiplash may produce marked pain and reduced mobility. More severe injuries require the person to adjust to life in a wheelchair, cope with facial or physical disfigurement and restricted movement.

Whiplash or acute neck strain is a common injury in accidents affecting about one third of sufferers. This is defined as soft tissue damage to the neck and shoulder caused by rapid forward and backward motion of the head on sudden stopping in a collision.

This injury to the neck occurs when:

- **You are unprepared for the impact.**
- **You are in a rear-end collision.**

Symptoms of whiplash are:

- **headache**
- **pain in the neck, shoulders or shoulder blades**
- **blurred vision**
- **dizziness**
- **concussion**
- **numbness**
- **altered sensations**
- **ringing in the ears (tinnitus).**

If you think you may be suffering from whiplash it is very important that you closely monitor the symptoms and consult your doctor as early as possible if you see no improvement.

PSYCHOLOGICAL CONSEQUENCES

Physical injuries also have a psychological component. As you attempt to deal with your injuries and the impact of the motor vehicle accident in general, psychological symptoms such as depression, anger and anxiety can set in. The psychological effects also have an impact on your physical recovery. Depression may lower your motivation to undergo or comply with rehabilitation instructions, and/or may lower pain thresholds. Depression and anxiety may also influence your rate of physical recovery following surgery.

Andrew B

Andrew, a 30-year-old carpenter, lost his leg below the knee as a result of a motorcycle accident. Despite his relatively satisfactory physical recovery he was plagued by continual pain.

He became increasingly depressed and socially isolated as a result of his pain and inability to walk properly. Although he attended a physiotherapy and rehabilitation program in the early stages after recovery, he became less and less inclined to make any effort to comply with his program as his depression worsened. He ceased to follow his rehabilitation instructions and eventually did not keep appointments. He began to become reliant on taking medication to ease the pain he was experiencing and was placed on anti-depressant medication.

Other psychological symptoms you may experience during and/or after the traumatic event include:
- **feelings of guilt and self-doubt**
- **feeling 'responsible'**
- **preoccupation with the trauma**
- **inability to continue working**
- **disruption to family and social life**
- **feeling vulnerable to future traumas**
- **a sense of insecurity.**

Grief is another important psychological reaction. It is a normal reaction and part of the recovery process. Grief and bereavement may follow the loss of a loved one, or some other type of loss. Common types of loss experienced after motor vehicle accidents include:
- **loss of a family member or friend**
- **physical or intellectual handicaps due to injury**
- **loss of employment and daily routine.**

Bereavements that are sudden and unexpected lead to greater stress for those who have perhaps lost a friend or a relative. It can also lead to greater difficulty in resolving and coming to terms with that loss.

When we are bereaved we may show this in a number of different ways. Some of the most common reactions are listed below.[5]

Feelings

- **sadness, crying**
- **pain at being separated from the person**
- **anger and frustration**
- **asking 'Why?' this happened**
- **guilt for (not) having done something**
- **anxiety**
- **loneliness**
- **fatigue**
- **helplessness**
- **shock**
- **intense yearning for the dead person**
- **numbness**

Physical sensations

- **hollowness in the stomach**
- **tightness in the chest**
- **lump in the throat**
- **dry mouth**
- **oversensitivity to noise**
- **a sense of depersonalisation**
- **shortness of breath**
- **weakness in muscles**
- **lack of energy**

Thoughts

- **disbelief**
- **confusion**
- **preoccupation with images of the dead person**
- **sense of presence**
- **hallucinations**

Behaviours/actions

- **difficulty sleeping**
- **loss of appetite**
- **forgetfulness**
- **social withdrawal**
- **dreams of the dead person**

- **avoiding reminders of the loss**
- **sighing**
- **disorganisation, poor concentration, restlessness**
- **visiting places or carrying objects or reminders of the deceased**
- **searching for any suggestion that the person might return**

Many people may not understand that what is happening to them is a normal process. They become distressed by their responses. Some fear that they are going insane, particularly if they can hear the voice, or feel the presence of the lost person. They may find that the image or the memory constantly keeps returning to their minds.

Some useful techniques to help you cope with loss can be to:
- **Write about the loss (keep a diary.**
- **Write a letter to the deceased person, expressing your thoughts and feelings toward them.**
- **Put together an album with photos or symbols to commemorate the deceased person.**
- **Draw or paint about your feelings (use different colours for different emotions).**

It is important to recognise the needs and rights of the grieving person. Many people find it helpful to view the deceased, to say their goodbyes and give last messages especially if the death has been sudden. It is also important that the survivors are involved in the planning of the funeral and activities surrounding it. This can help to give them a sense of control over the events and preparations. It is also important not to hurry the grieving person into disposing of the deceased's possessions. People often find it helpful to keep some things for months or even years before they are ready to let go.

- - - - - - - -
Remember

An emotional reaction to loss through traumatic circumstances is normal. This is not an illness. To help the normal grieving process resolve itself, it is important to talk about the loss of a relationship, and to express feelings of sadness, anger and sense of abandonment. The grieving process is a complex one and each person will come to terms with their emotions over different periods of time. For some it is done quickly and for others it may take several months. If the grief is intense and continues for several months or longer you may need to consult your general practitioner or community health centre for more assistance. There are also opportunities to seek help from bereavement counsellors who offer specialist services. Details on these may be available from your local community health centre or professional organisations such as the National Association for Loss and Grief (see the Appendix for a list of additional resources).

THE INTERACTION OF PSYCHOLOGICAL AND PHYSICAL FACTORS

Many of the reactions described above are not exclusive to loss. They can occur after any traumatic experience. Some of the most common are:

- **anxiety**
- **agitation**
- **restlessness**
- **depression**
- **withdrawal**
- **disorganisation**
- **sleep and appetite disturbances.**

It is important to remember that physical and psychological factors interact with each other in many ways, delaying recovery in one or both of these areas.

Physical and psychological elements interact so that:

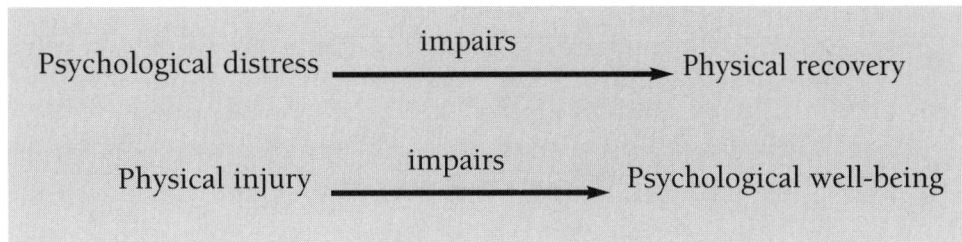

Psychological distress ———— *impairs* ————→ Physical recovery

Physical injury ———— *impairs* ————→ Psychological well-being

Not everyone encounters each of these experiences to the same degree, and there may be others added to the list. In most cases these experiences will subside over a short period of time, over a few hours, days or weeks, but in others they persist and interfere with our quality of life.

It is important to understand that there is no direct relationship between how severe the accident or injury was, and the severity or number of symptoms experienced. Even minor accidents and/or injuries can lead to problems. These reactions range in experience from a mild feeling of unease to a condition called Post-Traumatic Stress Disorder:

- *Mild*: **General feeling of fear or confusion about the accident.**
- *Specific symptoms*: **Sadness, guilt, nervousness, anger, fear.**
- *Symptom clusters*: **Depression, anxiety, avoidance of car travel, social withdrawal.**
- *Acute or Post-Traumatic Stress Disorder*: **Nightmares, flashbacks, ntrusive thoughts, avoidance, excessive physical arousal.**

An important point to note is that you can develop Post-Traumatic Stress Disorder (PTSD) if you have been personally involved in a trauma or if you have witnessed such a trauma. For example, if you were involved in a horrific car accident you may well develop PTSD. If an ambulance driver or police officer attends that accident they may also develop PTSD as a result of seeing the accident. PTSD, then, can be simple or complex in nature and can affect direct participants and/or observers.

Vicki M

Vicki, a 20-year-old university student, saw her boyfriend Greg hit by a truck as they attempted to cross a semi-busy road near her house. She was not hurt but Greg suffered bruising, a broken toe, fractured shoulder and two broken ribs. He made a reasonably quick recovery and went back to work about three months later putting the accident behind him.

Vicki, however, noticed that she became very emotional and teary every time she saw Greg, and began contemplating breaking off the relationship. She had dreams about the truck hitting Greg and at times she also saw herself being hit. She said she was becoming increasingly unhappy and no longer cared about her university studies. Where previously she was a good student, she was now just managing to pass. After much discussion with one of the counsellors at university she revealed that she felt responsible for Greg's accident as it had been her idea to cross the road at that time. She was plagued by feelings of guilt and sadness and had lost a considerable amount of weight in just a short period. She felt that she had no right to feel this way as she was not hurt but at the same time she could not help it.

George E

George, a 30-year-old member of a police rescue squad, was called to the scene of a fatal head-on collision just before midnight on a Sunday night. It had been raining earlier and the roads were slippery. The driver of one car had apparently fallen asleep at the wheel and his car had veered to the other side of the road. An oncoming car containing three young men was unable to get out of the way and collided head on. The driver who had fallen asleep behind the wheel died instantly. Later it was found that he had been drinking excessively.

Two of the young men in the other car were trapped for over one hour and came very close to dying. The third man had only minor injuries. George had attended many such scenes before and had always coped. But this time the young men reminded him of his own son in appearance. He started to see his own son as the accident victim. He began having flashbacks of the accident and nightmares where the trapped victims actually died before he could get them out of the car. He took time off work and began to drink to numb the memories. He became very withdrawn and was constantly irritable. His wife was very worried about him as he had always coped in the past.

2 POST-TRAUMATIC STRESS DISORDER

WHAT IS POST-TRAUMATIC STRESS DISORDER?

A person's response to a traumatic motor vehicle accident may vary in the number of symptoms recognised, their intensity and their duration. Even though stress reactions are common after a traumatic event, relatively few of these persist and develop into chronic Post-Traumatic Stress Disorder (PTSD). The majority of people who experience stress reactions in the first couple of weeks after the trauma spontaneously remit within the first few months.

Post-Traumatic Stress Disorder is a condition characterised by a group of specific symptoms. When diagnosing Post-Traumatic Stress Disorder, mental health professionals look for four major features or types of symptoms.

1 A person must have experienced, witnessed or been confronted with an event or number of events they have found to be horrifying, and which involved intense fear or helplessness in some way.

2 Distressing memories that come back frequently disturbing the person:
- **recurrent and *intrusive* memories that suddenly come into a person's mind and are difficult to get rid of**

and/or
- **repeated upsetting dreams or *nightmares***
- **sudden feelings that *events are actually happening again* — often called 'flashbacks'. These can occur at any time, even during waking periods.**

and/or
- **intense upset or *distress when faced with reminders of the event*.**

3 Because of the distress associated with the traumatic event people find themselves avoiding things that remind them of the event. For example, people may avoid:
- **thoughts or feelings associated with the trauma**
- **activities or situations that remind them of the trauma.**

or people may:
- **feel detached from others**
- **experience only a small range of emotions**
- **feel that they have no future.**

4 Persistent symptoms of increased arousal or physical tension.

It is important to understand that this description of PTSD is merely an outline of the major groups of symptoms that clinicians look for when diagnosing the condition. Clinicians use various sources of information and conduct very detailed interviews and assessments of clients in order to come to a diagnosis. They may interview family members, administer relevant questionnaires and consult other health professionals involved in treating the person.

In addition to the symptom clusters described above, one of the most distressing yet common sets of symptoms suffered after a trauma is that caused by excessive levels of physical arousal.

Symptoms of increased levels of physical arousal include:

- **trembling or shaking**
- **muscle tension, aches or pains**
- **restlessness and agitation**
- **shortness of breath**
- **palpitations**
- **sweating or cold clammy hands**
- **dry mouth**
- **dizziness or light headedness**
- **nausea, vomiting, diarrhoea, stomach pains**
- **hot flushes or chills**
- **frequent urination**
- **trouble swallowing—feeling of having a 'lump in the throat'.**

These symptoms may also show themselves through:

- **difficulty falling asleep or staying asleep**
- **irritability or outbursts of anger**
- **difficulty concentrating and short-term memory problems**
- **always watching for danger, feeling keyed up and on edge**
- **being often and easily startled by loud noises or sudden movements.**

PRACTICAL EXERCISE

Take a moment to think of the different types of symptoms you are experiencing. List all of these symptoms in the first column. In the spaces provided next to each symptom, write down the number of times you have experienced each of these symptoms.

Finally, rate the intensity of the worst episode of each symptom occurring in the last week. Use a ten point scale where a score of 10 represents an intensity of the symptom as being almost unbearable, and 1 where it is a minor feeling.

Minimal	Minor	Moderate	Severe	Unbearable
0 1	2 3	4 5 6	7 8	9 10

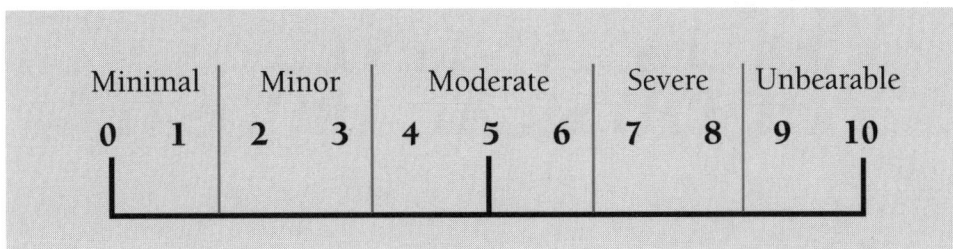

Symptom	Number of episodes in the last week	Intensity of symptom on the 10 point scale
Example: Having distressing dreams	4	Usually around 7
1		
2		
3		
4		
5		
6		
7		
8		
9		
10		
11		
12		

Recording the number and intensity of each symptom is important because you can use this information to see how you are progressing over time and what changes are being made. It also gives you a good guide as to which individual symptoms give you the most distress and which ones you can effectively deal with first.

3 DEALING WITH EXCESSIVE LEVELS OF PHYSICAL AROUSAL

INTRODUCTION

Individuals vary considerably in their responses to traumatic motor accidents. It is clear that such responses are not necessarily related to the severity of the accident. In some cases a seemingly 'minor' accident may be associated with a severe emotional reaction. In contrast, other people may show no obvious reaction following a 'major' accident involving serious injury.

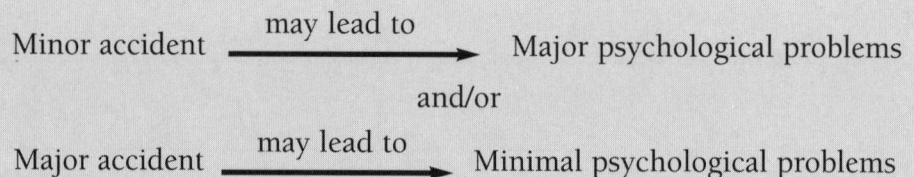

Minor accident ——— may lead to ———> Major psychological problems

and/or

Major accident ——— may lead to ———> Minimal psychological problems

What then are the factors that determine how a person will respond to an accident? They can be generally divided into two types: *vulnerability* and *protective* factors. **Vulnerability factors** are those things in a person's life, personality and experience that make them more likely to suffer emotional reactions. These factors may include:

- **poor social support**
- **anxious personality**
- **experience of previous trauma.**

Protective factors, on the other hand, as the name implies are those things that make a person more resilient or help them to bounce back after the motor vehicle accident, for example, good social support network.

Things that affect vulnerability and protective factors are associated with:

- *the trauma itself*: **the presence/absence of threat to life, exposure to unpleasant scenes, type and severity of injuries sustained, sense of personal responsibility**
- *the personality of the person*: **calm/anxious, secure/insecure, emotionally reactive/placid, physiologically easily/difficult to arouse**

- *early life-experiences*: sense of security/insecurity, extent of caring and stability of upbringing, previous exposure to traumas, previous emotional and psychiatric problems, drug and alcohol consumption
- *the present environment*: social isolation/support, family care, cultural issues, access to health and other services
- *the meaning of the incident/accident*: retribution.

A useful model in helping us understand how these factors and processes operate is shown in Figure 3.

Figure 3
A model for the development of PTSD

(Adapted from J.S. March (1990), The nosology of post-traumatic stress disorder, *Journal of Anxiety Disorders*, 4, 61–82)

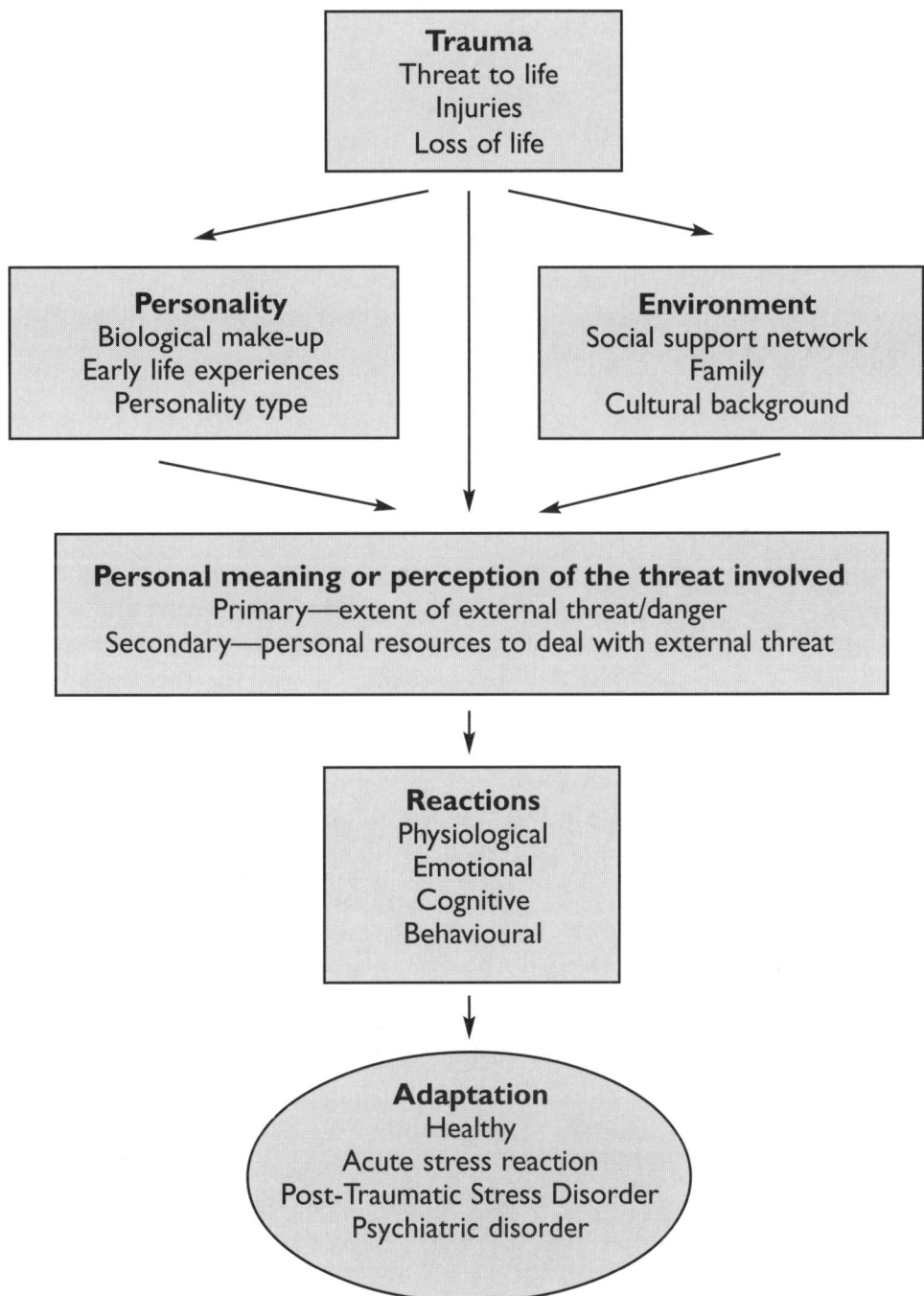

Trauma
Threat to life
Injuries
Loss of life

Personality
Biological make-up
Early life experiences
Personality type

Environment
Social support network
Family
Cultural background

Personal meaning or perception of the threat involved
Primary—extent of external threat/danger
Secondary—personal resources to deal with external threat

Reactions
Physiological
Emotional
Cognitive
Behavioural

Adaptation
Healthy
Acute stress reaction
Post-Traumatic Stress Disorder
Psychiatric disorder

Not all suggestions and skills will work for you. You may need to practice with these to see what works for you specifically. Trial and error are the keys to success.

It is clear that vulnerability and protective factors may be combined in a number of ways to influence a person's reaction to trauma.

Our early life experiences, our genetic and biological make-up, as well as our social background all determine how we interpret or appraise the meaning and consequences of the traumatic event. Ultimately it is our appraisal that determines whether the response will lead to emotional and psychiatric distress. Appraisal is the process by which a person evaluates the external danger or threat of an event (primary appraisal), and the personal resources available to deal effectively with that threat (secondary appraisal).

A person will have a negative appraisal of a situation if they believe that an external threat will be overwhelming, or that he/she lacks the necessary skills or ability to cope. This is compared with someone who appraises the threat as realistic but believes he/she can deal with any emotional stresses produced.

If you begin to engage in negative appraisal there is an increase in the probability that you will experience increased physiological arousal and emotional distress, that you will avoid distressing situations, possibly turn to drugs and/or alcohol, or begin to dwell on unpleasant and morbid thoughts.

These responses reflect the 'symptoms' of traumatic reactions. In the following chapters we will be describing four broad groups of traumatic stress reactions. These can be conveniently broken down into the following categories:

1   **physiological reactions**
2   **emotional reactions**
3   **cognitive reactions**
4   **behavioural reactions**

We will be taking each of these in turn and outlining various skills and techniques to help you overcome the distress caused by road trauma. Be aware that there is a great deal of interaction between the symptoms found in each category. For example, cognitive reactions have a specific and profound influence upon physiological reactions and vice versa.

We will give a brief description of the main features for each category. Then we will offer a number of different suggestions and practical behavioural ways of dealing with each of the symptoms found in that category.

PHYSIOLOGICAL REACTIONS
AROUSAL AND FEAR: THE 'FLIGHT OR FIGHT' RESPONSE

The 'flight or fight' response is a term used to describe our body's natural response to threat or danger. It is so named because all of its effects are aimed toward dealing with the threat by either fleeing or fighting the danger.

The flight or fight response is the most basic of emotional reactions and helped our evolutionary ancestors to survive and reproduce. When our ancestors recognised danger the nervous system in their brains 'switched on' to prepare their bodies to react in the best way to help get them out of immediate danger. Imagine you are crossing a street when suddenly you see a car speeding towards you. If you experience no anxiety you will most likely be hit by the car. However, your flight or fight response will 'switch on' and help you run out of the way to safety.

The flight or fight system is designed to protect us from harm. However, sometimes the flight or fight system cannot tell the difference between real or imagined danger, or between danger from outside the body (like the car), or inside the brain (like the memory of a traumatic event).

After a trauma the flight or fight system is switched on to any reminder of the trauma such as places, situations, sounds, smells, tastes, emotions, old memories or even bad dreams. Sometimes we are not even consciously aware of what it is that has triggered the flight or fight system.

For example, at times people describe a sudden sense of anxiety or panic when watching television. This concerns them because they cannot understand why, whilst relaxing in front of the TV, they should feel this way. What they are not consciously aware of is that the TV show may have the sound of an ambulance or police siren in the background or is showing a car chase/accident. This sound or sight acts as a reminder of their own trauma, causing a sudden rise in physical arousal and tension.

The most common physical signs and symptoms of high levels of arousal are:

- **faster heart beat**
- **sweating**
- **shaking**
- **paleness**
- **dizziness**
- **confusion**
- **quick breathing**
- **hot flushes**
- **numb feeling**
- **sense of unreality**
- **nausea**
- **light-headedness**
- **flushes**
- **tingling sensations in hands or feet**
- **weakness in the legs**
- **tightness and pains in the chest**
- **blurry vision**
- **rising panic.**

To better understand these physical reactions in your body, it is necessary to understand your body's physiological workings that control your energy levels and preparation for action.

The **autonomic nervous system** is the body's 'behind the scene' switchboard that *controls all automatic reactions* such as heart rate, sweating, digestion and eye-blinking. The system is a switchboard of nerves that receives messages from the brain, and whose role is to control the needs of the body. This system has two main operators:

- **the sympathetic nervous system**
- **the parasympathetic nervous system.**

THE SYMPATHETIC NERVOUS SYSTEM

The *sympathetic* part of the system controls the body's responses that occur during excitement or exertion. These are:

- **increased heart rate and strength of the heart beat**
- **increased blood flow**
- **increased speed and depth of breathing, including breathless ness, choking or smothering, pains or tightness in the chest**
- **unpleasant (but harmless) symptoms including dizziness, blurred vision, confusion, unreality and hot flushes**
- **decrease in salivation, resulting in a dry mouth.**

This is the flight/fight response where the body becomes ready for action. In the flight/fight mode adrenalin and noradrenaline chemicals are released from the glands in the kidneys. They are used as messengers by the sympathetic nervous system to trigger the release of other hormones.

The activity of the sympathetic nervous system continues until it is stopped in one of two ways:

- **by the action of the parasympathetic nervous system, or**
- **by other chemical messengers which destroy the adrenalin and noradrenaline that have been released.**

THE PARASYMPATHETIC NERVOUS SYSTEM

The *parasympathetic* nervous system acts against the effects of the sympathetic nervous system to bring the system back to normal. It is very important to realise that when aroused the body will eventually activate the parasympathetic nervous system to restore the normal state of arousal. In other words, anxiety cannot continue forever, nor can it spiral to ever increasing and possibly damaging levels.

Another important point is that the *chemical messengers*, adrenalin and noradrenaline, take some time to be destroyed. Thus, even after the danger has passed and your sympathetic nervous system has stopped responding, you are likely to feel keyed up or apprehensive for some time because the chemicals are still floating around in your system. You must remind yourself that this is perfectly natural and harmless.

Thus, the sympathetic nervous system is the flight or fight system which:

- **releases energy, and**
- **gets the body 'primed' for action.**

The parasympathetic nervous system is the restoring system that returns the body to a normal state.

BREATHING AND HYPERVENTILATION

When a person becomes aroused or anxious the rate and depth of breathing increases because the body's tissues need more oxygen. This increase in breathing is called hyperventilation. Survivors of a road trauma often experience intense anxiety when they are exposed to reminders of their accident or when they have to travel by motor vehicle. This anxiety causes a change in breathing rate and rhythm and leads to hyperventilation. To hyperventilate means to overbreathe, either too quickly or too deeply. Hyperventilation is also responsible for a number of other effects:

1   **The act of overbreathing is hard, physical work. So we may often feel hot, flushed and sweaty.**

2   **Because it is hard work to overbreathe, prolonged periods of tiredness and exhaustion will often result.**

3   **For those of us who overbreathe, we often tend to breathe from our chest rather than from our diaphragm. As the chest muscles are not made for breathing, they tend to become tired and tense. Thus we can experience symptoms of chest tightness or even severe chest pains.**

The efficient functioning of the human body depends on the proper balance between oxygen and carbon dioxide. The symptoms caused by hyperventilation are the result of depleted carbon dioxide in the blood. The balance can be restored through proper controlled breathing.

Overbreathing and hyperventilation can cause alarming sensations and their physical symptoms include:

- **dizziness**
- **confusion**
- **feeling faint**
- **flushing**
- **sweatiness**
- **nausea**
- **blurred vision**
- **faster heartbeat**
- **unreality.**

We will discuss ways to reduce these experiences later in the book.

HEART RATE AND BLOOD PRESSURE

Why do these symptoms arise? When you start to hyperventilate the blood oxygen to carbon dioxide ratio is altered. This results in a number of changes as the body attempts to return to its normal resting state. Although the biological mechanisms of these changes are complex, it is important to gain an understanding of these in order to realise that the symptoms you are experiencing are a *normal* part of the body's protective mechanism.

When the blood oxygen/carbon dioxide ratio is altered the oxygen molecules cling to the blood and are redirected to the vital internal organs. Because the oxygen is not readily released, the heart rate and blood pressure increase so that the oxygen can be transported quickly to where it is needed. This explains why you experience rapid heart beat.

Because blood is diverted to the internal organs and away from your hands and face, you go cold and pale, and you may feel tingling sensations in your lips and fingers or experience numbness. There may be an accompanying feeling of lightheadedness and dizziness. When this occurs, you feel as though you are about to faint. But remember, you will not faint. Why? Because the sympathetic nervous system acts to increase blood pressure. In order to faint, you need to have a sudden drop in blood pressure.

The lack of blood to certain muscles may cause pain, particularly in the chest and arms. This symptom, together with rapid heart beat (palpitations), sweatiness and breathlessness, cause many people to fear that they are having a heart attack.

Changes at the biochemical and molecular level result in an interference to fine muscular movement. This, together with trembling, means that smooth actions, such as writing and picking up objects, are carried out with difficulty.

The fears accompanying these sensations include:

- **a fear of having a heart attack or impending death**
- **a fear of fainting**
- **a fear of losing control and going berserk**
- **a fear of going insane.**

None of these occur. These sensations are not dangerous and can be brought under control by the techniques that will be practised. Overbreathing and hyperventilation are a normal and automatic response when we are anxious. They are protective devices signalling a threat.

We may not consciously recognise when we begin to hyperventilate because certain reminders of the accident remain subconscious. Therefore, awareness of the physical symptoms, such as those mentioned above, can alert us to the cause of our sense of discomfort or distress. With the anxiety management techniques that will be discussed shortly (such as breath control, relaxation, distraction techniques and thinking straight) we can regain control of our thoughts and fears and reduce the level of distressing physical reactions.

Nicole T

Nicole, a 45-year-old bank teller, was driving to work one morning when a car in the lane next to her suddenly changed lanes and collided with her car. She was not seriously injured but her car was damaged beyond repair.

She became very nervous every time she rode in a car and completely avoided driving. In addition, every time she saw a white station wagon (similar to the car that hit her) she became anxious, began to breathe quickly, her heart raced, she had chest pains, felt dizzy and thought she was going to pass out. She felt as though she was 'out of control' and wondered whether she was having a heart attack.

4

SKILLS TO REDUCE THE PHYSIOLOGICAL EFFECTS OF AROUSAL

The following techniques will not eliminate all post-trauma symptoms. They will help you gain control and cope with your emotional and physical stress reactions.

The skills taught here are called *anxiety management techniques* and are specifically aimed at reducing anxiety. They provide you with skills to directly control your physical arousal levels.

The techniques dealt with in this chapter are:
1 breathing retraining
2 relaxation training:

- **progressive muscle relaxation**
- **isometric relaxation**
- **release only relaxation**
- **cue-controlled relaxation**

3 distraction techniques
4 thinking straight.

All these techniques affect the autonomic nervous system to cause the sympathetic responses to slow down (that is, heart rate and breathing slow and blood pressure falls).

These techniques will:

- **help control your breathing**
- **reduce your level of arousal.**

BREATHING RETRAINING

This involves slowing down your breathing level. By breathing properly and making supportive, calming statements to yourself you can learn to manage panic.

> 1 **Begin by holding your breath for 10 seconds. *Do not* take a deep breath and then hold. Just stop and hold your breath.**
> 2 **Now slowly exhale to the count of 3 seconds ('one hundred, two hundred, three hundred').**
> 3 **Breathe in to the count of 3, hold for a second, then breathe out again to the count of 3 ('one hundred, two hundred, three hundred').**

Repeat the pattern described in steps 1 and 2.
NB: 1 second is the time it takes to say 'one hundred'.

The techniques are easy to learn and like learning anything new, the more you practise the better results you get.

Keep breathing in and out to the count of 3. Pace your breathing rate so that it takes 3 seconds to inhale and 3 seconds to exhale. Continue to do this for at least 1 minute.

If you still feel panicky, hold your breath for 10 seconds and repeat the exercise again. Continue doing this until the panic attack subsides.

RELAXATION TECHNIQUES

Regular use of relaxation techniques is a very useful way to unwind and maintain peace of mind. Regular practise of these techniques can help you feel calmer and more in control of your life. This is important for confidence and self-esteem. The aim of relaxation is to enable you to achieve a state of physical and mental ease.

There are various ways of learning relaxation techniques. Although not described here, meditation and yoga are very effective techniques. Training groups for these are available in the community and are advertised in local newspapers.

We will describe several simple techniques here. If necessary, these can be supplemented by commercially available relaxation audio-cassette tapes.

PROGRESSIVE MUSCLE RELAXATION

When your muscles are tense you feel 'uptight'. Muscle tension tends to restrict your breathing. When your breathing is shallow and restricted you are more likely to experience anxiety.

You may have noticed that when your body is tense your mind has a greater tendency to 'race'. As you relax the muscles throughout your body your mind will begin to slow down and become calmer.

A relaxed body results in a relaxed mind. This approach involves consciously relaxing the large muscles of your body. Progressive muscle relaxation means that the muscles are relaxed in an orderly sequence, usually starting with the leg and foot muscles and ending with the hands and arms.

Now, find a comfortable quiet place to sit and see that you will not be interrupted for about 20 minutes.

Relaxation instructions

1 Close your eyes and focus on your breathing, keeping it slow and even. Say the word 'relax' to yourself as you breathe out.

2 Tense up your right foot, squeezing your toes together and pointing them downwards. Focus on that tension. Slowly release that tension as you breathe out, saying the word 'relax' to yourself.

3 Now tense up your calf muscle and hold the tension for a while. Slowly release the tension as you breathe out.

4 Go through the other muscles in your body, working through the muscles of your right leg, left leg, buttocks, back, abdomen, chest, shoulders, left arm and fingers, right arm and fingers, neck, jaw, lips, eyes and forehead.

5 When you finish 'scan' through your body and make sure that most of the tension has been released. If some areas are still tense you can spend extra time just relaxing those places.

6 Slowly open your eyes and try to maintain that feeling of relaxation for the rest of the day.

While you are learning the progressive muscle relaxation technique, it is recommended that you practise at least twice a day to get the full benefit of the exercise.

ISOMETRIC RELAXATION

Isometric relaxation exercises are used when you experience fear. They are useful for remaining relaxed at times when you actually confront your fears. Progressive muscle relaxation exercises are useful for becoming relaxed before and after you confront your fears. Most isometric relaxation exercises do not involve any obvious change in posture or movement. This is because 'isometric' refers to exercises in which the length of the muscle remains the same. Isometric exercises involve controlling the muscles whilst the body remains still. Because the muscle stays the same length there is no obvious movement.

The following exercises are meant to be gentle and slow. The aim is to relax you.

When sitting in a public place[6]

1   **Take a breath, let it go and slowly count to 7 before taking another breath. At the same time slowly tense leg muscles by crossing your feet at the ankles and press down with the upper leg while trying to lift the lower leg.**

    or

    After taking a breath, let it go and then slowly count to 7, slowly saying the word 'relax' to yourself.

2   **Let all the tension go from your muscles.**

3   **Close your eyes.**

4   **For the next minute each time you breathe out, saying the word 'relax' to yourself, and let all the tension flow out of your muscles.**

Choose other parts of the body to relax, eg. the hands and arms.

1   **Take a breath, let it go and slowly count to 7 before taking another breath.**

2   **At the same time tense your hand and arm muscles by placing your hands comfortably in your lap, palm against palm, and pressing down with the top hand while trying to lift the lower hand.**

    or

    Place hands under the sides of the chair and pull into the chair.

    or

    Grasp hands behind the chair and try to pull them apart while simultaneously pushing them in against the back of the chair.

    or

    Place hands behind your head, interlocking the fingers and, whilst pushing head backward into hands, try to pull hands apart.

3   **After taking a breath, let it go and then slowly count to 7... Slowly say the word 'relax' to yourself... Let all the tension go from your muscles... Close your eyes... For the next minute each time you breathe out say the word 'relax' to yourself and let all the tension flow from your muscles... If circumstances permit continue with various muscle groups.**

When standing in a public place

1 Take a breath, let it go and slowly count to 7 before taking another breath.

2 At the same time straighten legs to tense all muscles, bending the knees back almost as far as they will go.

3 After taking a breath, let it go and then slowly count to 7, slowly saying the word 'relax' to yourself.

4 Let all the tension go from your muscles.

5 Close your eyes.

6 For the next minute each time you breathe out say the word 'relax' to yourself and let all the tension flow from your muscles.

Other exercises for hand and arm muscles

1 Take a breath, let it go and slowly count to 7 before taking another breath.

2 At the same time cup hands together in front of you and try to pull them apart.

or

Cup hands together behind you and try to pull them apart.

or

Tightly grip an immovable rail or bar and feel the tension in your arms.

3 After taking a breath, let it go and then slowly count to 7, slowly saying the word 'relax' to yourself.

4 Let all tension go from your muscles.

5 Close your eyes.

6 For the next minute each time you breathe out say the word 'relax' to yourself and let all the tension flow from your muscles.

Just before you breathe out say 'relax' to yourself.

RELEASE ONLY RELAXATION (5–7 MINUTES)

This relaxation technique is intended to help you lessen the time it takes you to relax by not using the tension approach.

Start by using breathing relaxation and try to relax as much as possible while doing this. Relaxation will begin from the top of your head and move through your body to the tip of your toes. If you find that a particular part of your body is difficult to relax, tense it and let it go.

Breathe with calm, regular breaths and feel yourself relaxing more and more with every breath... • just let go... • relax your forehead... •eyebrows... • eyelids... • jaws... • tongue and throat... • your entire face... • relax your neck... • shoulders... • arms... • and all the way down to your finger tips... • continue to breathe calmly and regularly with your stomach... • let the feeling of relaxation spread to your stomach... • waist and back... • relax the lower part of your body, your bottom... • thighs... • knees... • calves... • feet... • and all the way down to the tip of your toes... • breathe calmly and regularly and feel how you relax more and more with each breath... • take a deep breath and hold it for a couple of seconds... • and let the air out slowly... • slowly... • notice how you relax more and more.

If a particular muscle group proves difficult to relax, briefly tense it and then release it again.

CUE-CONTROLLED RELAXATION

Cue-controlled relaxation involves talking to yourself whilst doing breathing relaxation. In other words, you relax yourself by 'cuing' your breathing rate with the word 'relax'. Once you have mastered this you will be able to relax during normal everyday activities without taking too much time. The method sounds simple but again it takes practice.

PRACTICAL EXERCISE

Select a particular relaxation strategy that you feel comfortable using. In the space provided below start recording every time you attempt a particular relaxation technique.

While learning these techniques it is suggested that you practise at least a few times a day to get the full benefit of them. Use this self-monitoring form to remind yourself of the exercise and to keep track of your progress.

Date	Time	Type of relaxation	How helpful was it?

5 DEALING WITH EMOTIONAL REACTIONS

Many emotions are felt by people involved in a motor vehicle accident. These can be very confusing and cause considerable distress. The immediate response to an accident may be numbness and shock. As time goes on, the person may start to react by being particularly irritable, frustrated and angry over minor irritations, or feel generally apprehensive, agitated or anxious. There may also be feelings of guilt or depression and a lack of an ability to enjoy previously pleasurable activities.

Immediate response

- *Numbness*: **You may feel as if the accident never happened, as if it were a bad dream.**
- *Shock*: **You seem to be in a daze, feel isolated or detached from other people, and your surroundings and even people seem unreal.**

Later responses

- *Anger*: **This could be towards yourself or others. Questions such as 'Why me?', 'What did I do to deserve this?', 'What is happening to me?', 'Am I falling apart?' are common. Anger comprises a continuum of emotions ranging from rage to impatience and irritation. Frustration is perhaps the most common form of anger that most of us experience.**
- *Fear*: **This could be fear of being left alone; a fear that you think you are losing control of yourself; a fear of a similar event happening again; feeling vulnerable.**
- *Guilt*: **Blaming yourself for what happened. Feeling guilty or 'responsible' for another person's death. Feeling guilty about having done certain things or acted in some way that might have led to the accident occurring.**
- *Depression*: **Feelings of isolation and a sense of being alone. Having no sense of purpose and feeling helpless.**

What we must realise is that emotional reactions are strongly influenced by our level of arousal and our thoughts and beliefs. For example, people and situations do not, in themselves, always have to make us angry; it is our interpretation of what others do and say and how we interpret this that leads us to react with anger.

Anger and depression may perhaps be two of the most difficult emotions you will have to face. Let us focus firstly on anger.

ANGER

Anger is one of the most troubling emotions associated with a post-trauma reaction. Anger, like anxiety or pain, is a stress reaction. It is problematic because it makes us:

- **less able to tolerate frustration**
- **more irritable and cranky**
- **cause arguments with others**
- **want to avoid socialising with others**
- **turn to alcohol or drugs to try and settle down**
- **do and say things we may later regret**
- **become isolated from others.**

If the anger is directed inwards, then:

- **we act in a self-defeating manner**
- **if depressed, we may harm ourselves or attempt suicide**
- **we feel worthless and dislike ourselves.**

Henry K

Henry, a 28-year-old married accountant with three children, was involved in a minor rear end collision. He was stationary at the time when he looked into his rear view mirror to see a vehicle approaching at speed. He realised instantly that the vehicle would not stop in time and braced himself for the impact. He sustained a whiplash injury but no other major injuries. The whiplash injury resulted in constant headaches and restricted his head movements, thus preventing him from participating in sporting activities. He was a keen competitive squash player. In addition, he was unable to carry our his work duties and was placed on sick leave.

With time, he became increasingly agitated and angry at being an innocent victim of someone else's negligent behaviour and having his whole life turned upside down. He felt a sense of injustice. He became increasingly resentful and bitter at his predicament. His irritation was taken out on others through sarcasm, verbal outbursts and intolerance for any frustration. He became irritated by the noise his children made, their constant demands and need for attention, and would scream at them to leave him alone. People began to avoid his company and his wife was on constant guard not to upset him. His alcohol consumption increased, further aggravating his irritable mood.

It is important to acknowledge and recognise that anger, as is the case with all our emotions, can serve a useful purpose in our lives. However, real anger really only lasts for a short time. If it lasts longer it may be tapping into some unresolved anger from the past, and may change into resentment, bitterness, or depression. Physical tension, negative thoughts and perceptions can often exacerbate the anger response and cause people to express this emotion in inappropriate ways, for example, domestic violence, damage to property and alcohol abuse.

It is important to:

- **recognise the detrimental effects that the inappropriate expression of anger can have, and**
- **re-direct the energy and emotion that anger can generate into more appropriate means of expression.**

TENSION

If you are feeling uptight for any reason, you are more likely to respond to situations with anger, situations which you otherwise would have shrugged off as minor irritations and dismissed as not worth getting uptight about. When aroused we become irritated by small things like noise, lights, movement, crowds and people making repeated demands on us.

THOUGHTS

Thoughts are also important. If we believe that others are taking advantage of us, doing things deliberately to annoy us or acting toward us in an unfair or threatening way, we will respond with anger.

PERCEPTIONS

Another important issue is the frustration and anger caused by the perception that organisations such as employer groups, insurance companies or doctors are not really providing enough recognition or assistance in dealing with the aftermath of an accident. Often survivors feel that the only concern employers have is that the person returns to work as quickly as possible to minimise costs to the company, and for the insurance company it is to avoid compensation payouts. Survivors often believe that doctors dismiss or fail to appreciate the severity of their accidents and the impact on their quality of life. Survivors become bitter and angry toward the 'system'. In some cases this anger becomes all encompassing, resulting in their total preoccupation with the effects of the accident.

To reduce this anger it is necessary to change the perception that it is a 'me' against 'them' situation. There is no such thing as a 'system' but rather individuals working according to rules and procedures which they have little opportunity to bypass. For example, part of the insurance assessor's job is to make sure all claims are genuine. Even though the assessor may believe in the truth of a sufferer's description, he/she is still required to obtain objective evidence from other sources, such as a doctor's report.

This is the procedure the assessor must follow irrespective of his/her own beliefs. However, from the sufferer's viewpoint this action represents just another example of the 'system' trying to avoid its obligation. It is therefore important to place other people's actions in proper perspective.

The purpose of this section is to increase your ability to:

- **anticipate situations that may provoke anger**
- **apply techniques to help control the level of anger experienced**
- **express the anger in socially acceptable ways**
- **feel confident in doing so, and**
- **feel good about yourself for having achieved the above.**

When confronted with an anger-inducing situation two types of reactions immediately come into effect:

- **your level of physical arousal increases (your heart rate increases, you become tense and prepared for action), and**
- **certain negative thoughts enter your mind.**

In anger the body prepares to act by attacking the source of frustration, threat or danger. This leads to muscle tension, rigid body posture, reddening of the face, flaring of the nostrils and heavy breathing. You have already learnt techniques to reduce your level of arousal. Use one of these techniques here. Relaxation techniques can be applied immediately when:

- **you anticipate exposure to a frustrating or threatening situation**
- **you start to notice warning cues that your level of anger is about to increase**
- **you feel angry.**

Once you have expressed your anger, relaxation is also effective in bringing you back to your normal resting level of arousal. This means that you are less likely to brood and it may make you less likely to respond to further aggravation.

THE PROCESS OF LITIGATION

Going through a compensation litigation procedure can be a difficult process. This is because of the uncertainty of what needs to be done and when, and the complexity of associated legal requirements. How satisfied we are with regard to what is happening depends on how much we understand what is going on and how involved we are during the case and its outcome.

The way in which the system is structured means that often a person will need to visit a number of doctors for assessment. Some doctors act on behalf of the insurance companies and others for the solicitor representing the client. At times a person may feel not enough is being done or that organisations are interested more in the financial aspects of litigation than the well-being of the victim. This often generates feelings of resentment and anger at the process and system in general. People become irritable and hostile toward professionals assessing them.

Remember, however, that the 'system' has been created to ensure that people receive their due compensation and do not miss out. It is also there to make sure that no-one takes unfair advantage of the system. Safeguards must be put in place. This unfortunately may cause irritation to the majority who are genuine cases in need.

Keep in mind, there is no such thing as a 'system' that is against you specifically, but rather individuals trying to do their job. Being angry and bitter will not help matters but will only increase the risk of irritating yourself. It may also prolong your recovery process. Just keep in mind that the solicitor is the first and last point of contact you will have with the legal system. It is through them that your case is constructed, conducted and finalised.

The first step to take is to understand what is involved in a litigation process. This will help you to decrease any unnecessary anxiety that may surface.[7]

There are six aspects to the litigation process. In each of these aspects we shall give you personal accounts of how others have found the system. The legal profession is not positively perceived by some of the public.

1 Case duration: the time between the commencement of the case and its finalisation
   'I think it is appalling that my case began in May 1980 and was resolved and awarded in July 1993.'
2 The method used to resolve the claim
   'I would have liked to be involved more in the negotiations instead of being left isolated as if it didn't concern me, until the settlement was agreed. That's how I experienced it all.'

3 Compensation received
'Money is important, but it's not all. It can't buy me back my health, my job and the way I used to be...'

4 Lawyers' fees and other charges
'Yes, he sure knows how to charge for the smallest of things, like pencils, photocopies etc.'

5 Information provided by your lawyer
'Don't keep everything so secretive—humanise the system.'
'More information on the way the Supreme Court works and my lawyers and my participation in the court.'

6 What your experience with the Supreme Court is to date: how informed you are about the general procedures of the court
'How the system works and what is expected from you, most people are very nervous in matters like this.'
'On every aspect—what to expect! What may happen, what choices I have to make, just generally tell me what to do—if and when to be of assistance, not let me feel I was being thrown into something so alone.'

From these comments we see that many of the concerns arise out of common litigation experiences. These examples show that the various stages of the litigation process were often inadequately dealt with in terms of amount of information given to the concerned parties.

When we think of a client-lawyer relationship, often what comes to mind is that the 'professional role is to assume broad control over solutions to the problem brought in by the client'. This may be soothing for us in the beginning.

What we must realise is that having a say in what is happening to our case is often better than passively letting someone take 'control' of our situation. This only results ultimately in us becoming lost as to how the system actually operates once the wheel starts to turn. It is likely that if our expectations are not met, we may get resentful and distrusting towards the legal system that is doing its best to be as fair as possible.

PRACTICAL
EXERCISE

Here are some questions you may need to ask yourself every once in a while to make sure that you are on top of the whole case.

- **When you first saw your lawyer, about how long did he/she say it would take to get compensation for your personal injury case? Did you have any expectations about the likely outcome?**

- **Do you have any concerns about the method used so far to resolve your case? How involved were you during the whole proceedings? How comfortable are you feeling about what is happening around you?**

Allow yourself to play an important role in these proceedings; have your say in what is going on.

- **Before you saw your lawyer, did you have any idea how much money you might get? Was your expectation realistic?**

- **Are there any concerns that you may have about your lawyer's fees or any other charges at present?**

- **How well informed has your lawyer kept you about the progress of your case?**

- **Do you feel that you have understood how your case has been conducted? Was there anything about the procedures that were unclear to you? Is it too late to do something about it?**

STEPS TO TAKE IN DEALING WITH ANGER

1 Apply relaxation techniques	• Reduce tension • Distract attention from trigger • Provide time to think of an alternative response.
2 Apply cognitive procedures	• Ask yourself specific questions: Is there something constructive I can do about this? Why am I becoming angry? Am I reading the situation correctly or is there another interpretation possible? What do I hope to achieve by being angry? Is it really worthwhile to get angry? • Ask yourself: If I do respond with anger now, what are the consequences later on?
3 Rehearse self-statements[8] a) *Preparing for provocation*	• This is going to upset me, but I know how to deal with it. • There won't be any need for an argument. • Try to keep this in perspective. • Time for a few deep breaths of relaxation. Feel comfortable, relaxed and at ease.
b) *Impact and confrontation*	• Stay calm. Just continue to relax. • What do I want to get out of this? • Look for the positives. Don't assume the worse or jump to conclusions. • I'm on top of this situation and it's under control.
c) *Coping with arousal*	• My muscles are starting to feel uptight. Time to relax and slow things down. • Getting upset won't help. • Try to reason it out. Treat each other with respect. • Negatives lead to more negatives. Work constructively.
d) *When conflict is unresolved*	• Forget the aggravation. Thinking about it only makes me upset. • Remember relaxation. It's a lot better than anger.
e) *When conflict is resolved or coping is successful*	• That wasn't as hard as I thought. • I could have been more upset than it was worth.

PRACTICAL EXERCISE

Over the next few days identify a situation that has made you angry. Write down in detail the things that led up to the episode, what happened and how you handled it. Now write down what thoughts you had at each of these points in time.

Evaluate the situation by asking the following questions:

- **What was the problem?**
- **What led to it?**
- **Could I have seen it coming?**
- **What really made me angry? Did I feel devalued, criticised, threatened or made to feel a fool, etc?**
- **What did I do?**
- **What else could I have done? Left the scene (time-out), not say anything, etc?**
- **Was it really worth getting upset and angry about? Did I achieve an outcome that benefited me?**
- **Next time a similar situation arises, what is the best way of handling it?**

Draw up a list like the one shown below and over the next few days write down the problem that has made you angry and how you handled it.

Problem
What led to it?
What has made me angry about this problem?
What did I do?
What else could I have done?

DEPRESSION

Depression is another response that you may experience after what has happened to you.

Depression is often found as a common feature of anxiety and other stress conditions. With these constant feelings of anxiety you may feel frustrated and depressed, fearing that you will never overcome these problems. As the depression worsens you may start to see things that happen in their environment or to you in more negative ways. With this comes increased negative feelings about yourself and your ability to handle stress. As a result your anxiety also worsens.

To be able to cope effectively with depression, it is important to understand what depression is and how it interacts with anxiety.

WHAT IS DEPRESSION?

Depression is a normal human emotion in which there is an experience of:

- **low mood**
- **sadness**
- **loss of energy**
- **blame**
- **loss of interest**
- **loss of motivation**
- **low self-esteem**
- **feelings of guilt and hopelessness.**

The severity of depression may vary considerably, ranging from mild through to intense emotions of despair and despondency.

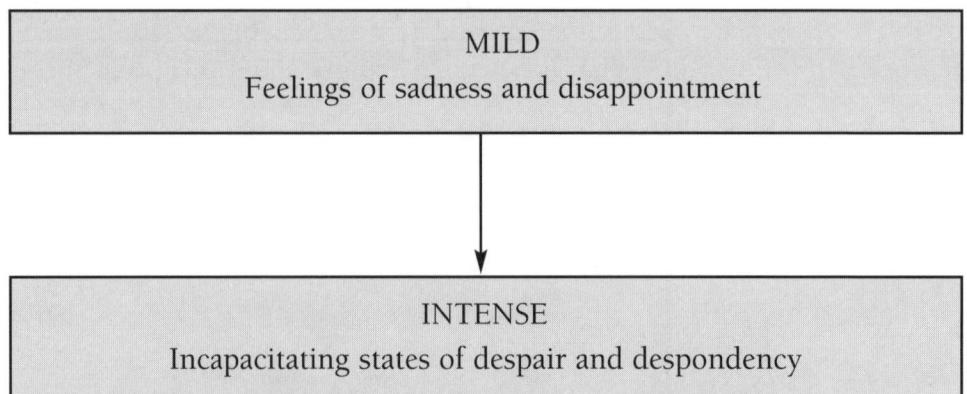

```
┌─────────────────────────────────────────────────┐
│                      MILD                         │
│       Feelings of sadness and disappointment      │
└─────────────────────────────────────────────────┘
                          │
                          ▼
┌─────────────────────────────────────────────────┐
│                    INTENSE                        │
│    Incapacitating states of despair and despondency │
└─────────────────────────────────────────────────┘
```

The depression may be reactive, triggered by environmental stress, or may arise seemingly spontaneously due to biochemical influences (these will be explained in detail later in the chapter).

There is no single factor to explain the onset of depression. Rather, it is the end result of the interaction of a number of factors, including:

- **biological make-up**
- **past history**
- **environment**
- **social/family support.**

SYMPTOMS OF DEPRESSION

Depression comprises a group of symptoms that affect a number of mental and physical functions. While a common core of symptoms exists, individuals experience variations in the pattern and intensity of their symptoms.

The main areas of functioning affected by depression are:

- ***Affective*: Low mood, irritability, lack of enjoyment in activities, emotional deadness, anxiety, emptiness.**
- ***Motivational*: Absence of motivation, lack of effort, procrasti nation, no sense of purpose, lack of sense of achievement, lethargy, fatigue.**
- ***Behavioural*: Withdrawal, poor tolerance for frustration, frequent crying spells, use of alcohol or drugs, slowness of behaviour, agitation—wringing hands, reduced speech.**
- ***Somatic*: Aches and pains, gastric problems—constipation, diarrhoea, anorexia, weight loss, excessive eating, insomnia, early morning awakening, excessive sleep, reduced sexual interest, feeling 'off', fatigue.**
- ***Cognitive*: Thoughts of self-worthlessness, guilt, self-blame, low self-esteem, low self-confidence, bleak view of the future, feeling helpless and out of control, suicidal thoughts, overly self-critical.**

The clinical disorder of depression has been classified into subgroups, in particular, reactive and biological types of depression.

REACTIVE DEPRESSION

As the term implies reactive depression develops in reaction or response to environmental stress. For example, the unexpected loss of employment due to the injuries sustained during the accident results in depression which may disappear within a relatively short time once the stress is resolved.

The main characteristics of this type of depression are as follows:

- **Depressed mood may fluctuate and respond to external influences but does not entirely disappear.**
- **Feelings of apathy, loss of interest in work and recreation arise.**
- **There is a loss of self-esteem and confidence.**
- **The ability to make rational decisions is reduced or distorted.**
- **Anxiety symptoms may emerge.**

BIOLOGICAL DEPRESSION

Biological depression is a severe form of depression that, as the name implies, 'comes from within'. Biological depression may or may not be precipitated by external stresses. It is often referred to as biological depression because of the evidence of biochemical changes and genetic links.

The symptom pattern includes:

- **marked depressed mood**
- **lack of reactivity**
- **depressive delusions**
- **guilt**
- **loss of changes**
- **changes in sleep**
- **changes in appetite**
- **changes in weight.**

SECONDARY DEPRESSION

Depression may also be associated with the symptoms of another medical or psychiatric condition. For example, physical injuries, physical illnesses such as viral infections, cancer and neuromuscular disorders (Parkinson's disease, multiple sclerosis) may produce depression.

Some drugs, either prescribed or non-prescribed, may produce depression. Alcohol is a depressant. Some anti-hypertensive drugs, designed to reduce blood pressure, may provoke depressive episodes. Often people suffering from anxiety develop depression as a secondary consequence to their fears.

If you are suffering depression consult your local general practitioner or community health centre for advice regarding medication and further specific techniques to help you cope.

PRACTICAL
EXERCISE

When you experience episodes of depression write down the symptoms, the thoughts that run through your mind and what you plan to do about these emotions. Be as accurate and truthful as possible as this exercise is for your benefit. Be active in keeping a record of these episodes.

Symptom	My thoughts	My actions
eg. Irritability	eg. I'm worthless	eg. I shouldn't have such high expectations of myself. I'm not worthless, what I'm attempting to do is just a little beyond me. What other ways can I go about this?

6 DEALING WITH COGNITIVE REACTIONS

Thinking about an unpleasant situation can affect the way we feel and behave. We can make those feelings worse by dwelling on those thoughts and by imagining in elaborate detail all the things that could go wrong. To illustrate this more clearly let us look back on the topic of depression and talk about the cognitive factors involved in depression.

COGNITIVE FACTORS OF DEPRESSION

Symptoms of depression arise out of the manner in which we negatively evaluate ourselves in terms of:

- **current experiences**
- **the future.**

When we are depressed we see ourselves as worthless, inadequate or at fault. Because of an over-critical and negative evaluation of our own skills and qualities we begin to lose self-esteem and self-confidence.

Associated with this negative self-view is the tendency to experience events around us in a negative way. Activities lose their sense of enjoyment and appeal, work is seen as demanding and hostile, and insurmountable obstacles are seen as deliberately placed in our way. Nothing is seen as worthwhile pursuing because of the 'knowledge' that it is certain to fail.

As a consequence the future appears bleak and pessimistic. There is no point in attempting anything because we believe everything will turn out poorly. Any long-term plans are expected to meet with frustration and failure. Why should we pursue them when there will be no ultimate pleasure or sense of achievement. Apathy sets in.

As a result we lose motivation to act, overestimate the difficulty of normal tasks and become dependent on others whom we perceive as more competent and deserving.

Where do these negative thoughts originate?

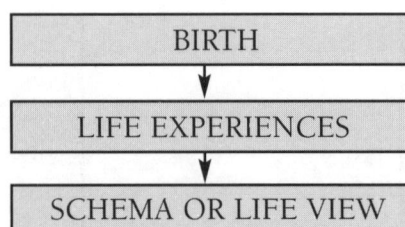

```
        BIRTH
          ↓
    LIFE EXPERIENCES
          ↓
   SCHEMA OR LIFE VIEW
```

From birth, we are inundated with stimuli and information from our environment. In order to make some sense of the world, all this information needs to be received, filtered, systematically arranged and organised into some sort of manageable whole. **Schema** represent the means by which this is achieved.

Negative thinking styles are learnt. They are based on our upbringing, our early experiences and often our unwillingness to explore the rationality of these thoughts. Newer, positive rational ways of thinking are also learnt. They depend on recognising and correcting faulty thinking styles so that a person can learn to reduce depression and stress.

There are many different types of faulty thinking styles which can systematically lead to an increase in depression. Many of these thinking styles lead to thoughts that appear to arise 'automatically', that is, they come almost without our (conscious) awareness. We do not realise that we are thinking in these particular negative styles. A good analogy is that of the habit of driving a motor vehicle. With so much practice we are able to change gears and direction while judging the speed of oncoming cars at the same time as talking to the passenger. These acts are carried out so habitually that we do them 'automatically' without conscious thought. This is the same with our negative thinking styles so that we are no longer aware that we are doing so.

Below are examples of negative or unrealistic thinking styles:

- *All or nothing thinking*: **Everything is seen in black and white.**

  (eg. I cannot return to work until I am 100 percent recovered.)

- *Over-generalisation*: **assuming the same behaviour from a group based on the actions of an individual.**

  (eg. I am a burden on my family and friends because they have to drive me everywhere.)

- *Mental filter*: **Focusing on a negative aspect of a situation.**

  (eg. I nearly died in the accident, I came so close.)

- *Jumping to conclusions*: **Making assumptions about what others are thinking regarding your reactions to the trauma.**

  (eg. Everyone thinks I am making a big deal out of nothing.)

- *Magnification and minimisation*: **Highlighting your weaknesses and minimising your strengths.**

  (eg. I am hopeless, every time I have to go somewhere I get really nervous. I always keep appointments and am on time but I should be able to cope better and not get so nervous.)

- *'Should statements'*: **Using judgmental words such as 'should', 'must', 'have to' inappropriately.**

  (eg. I should be able to cope. I must stop crying all the time.)

- *Personalisation*: **Assuming blame for what happened.**

  (eg. If I had gone a different way the accident would not have happened.)

LEARNING TO IDENTIFY NEGATIVE THOUGHTS

Because many negative thoughts are 'automatic' you may not be fully aware of them. You need to learn the skill of identifying the presence and nature of these thoughts, especially those related to depression. There are a number of ways of doing this:

1   **Listen to the way you talk to yourself in your head. Listen to the harsh, critical, nagging, hassling thoughts. Write them down.**

2   **Set 15 minutes aside each evening. Recall specific events that have occurred during the day.**

3   **Write down the thoughts you had prior to and after the event. Record any upsetting thoughts as accurately as you can. The most accurate way of recording negative cognitions is to record them as soon as they occur. If you experience an upsetting thought jot it down immediately for later reference.**

4   **Spend time identifying periods or situations during the day in which your depression is worse. What are your thoughts prior to or during this time?**

To become more aware of the relationship and pattern of negative cognitions on mood and behaviour, monitor your thoughts over a one week period. Your record should include the following:

Day	Event (Event or thinking about event that led to unpleasant emotions)	Feeling (Specify: sad, angry, guilty. Rate intensity 0–100 percent)	Cognition (Write down specific thoughts)

With decreased activity comes increased brooding.

HOW TO RE-MOTIVATE YOURSELF

- - - - - - - - - - - - - - - -

The downward spiral

The process of depression leads to a cycle of worsening mood and inactivity. As depression sets in everything becomes an effort to do, you fatigue easily and lose enjoyment and satisfaction of those things that you do manage to do. With increased tiredness comes lethargy and this may result in avoidance behaviours such as social withdrawal or procrastination. As your level of activity decreases so does the number of sources of potential satisfaction or enjoyment. When you do nothing the habit of doing nothing gives you satisfaction and this brings your mood down. Finally, the actual effort of attempting to do something becomes too much.

People function best, and their mood improves, when they receive positive reinforcement or rewards for their achievements.

Positive reinforcement may come from:

- **others praising or complimenting our efforts**
- **personal satisfaction of achieving our goals**
- **intrinsic enjoyment gained from participation in an activity.**

Often just engaging in an activity such as visiting friends, going to the movies or taking up a hobby gives a sense of an enjoyment that may lead you to look forward to doing it again in the near future.

Therefore, the number and source of potentially reinforcing activities are dependent upon how active you are in actually doing something. The more you do the more likely you are to reap the benefits of positive reinforcement.

Remember, when you are depressed:

- **You lose interest and find it difficult to muster enough energy to get going.**
- **As you lose interest you become pessimistic, and you begin to view the future bleakly and do not expect to receive any positive reinforcement from doing things.**
- **As you do less you start avoiding or not meeting your responsibilities. You start feeling guilty about letting people down.**
- **As you let people down you invite criticism from others. You start blaming and criticising yourself, regarding yourself as worthless and blameworthy. Your self-esteem, self-confidence and sense of personal adequacy diminishes. You withdraw socially.**
- **You start to lose skills necessary to carry out or accomplish tasks or to engage in interactions with others.**
- **Anger and irritability arise out of frustration or the perception that people have rejected or blamed you. You may start taking that anger out on yourself or others.**

- -

WHY DO PEOPLE NEED TO BECOME MORE ACTIVE?

Certain benefits are associated with increased activity levels:

- **Your mood may be improved through distraction from negative thoughts. Concentrating on a task will shift your focus or attention away from yourself and your problems towards something that is more enjoyable and positive.**
- **Doing things may provide you with a sense of control or achievement over your environment.**
- **Paradoxically, you may feel less tired. With depression you feel lethargic and exhausted and doing nothing will only worsen that feeling. By becoming active you 'pep yourself up', and with physical exercise your concentration and physical condition improves, allowing you to do things with less effort and more enjoyment. Increased physical activity may also lead to a better quality of sleep. Therefore, the more you do the more you feel like doing.**

BARRIERS TO BECOMING ACTIVE

Negative thoughts are the main barriers to becoming motivated. With depression, pessimistic thoughts lead us to question the value, purpose or sense of doing anything. Thoughts such as:

'Its no use, I'll probably fail again.'
'It won't work out the way I want it to.'
'No-one will appreciate my efforts.'
'Why bother doing it, it won't last.'

will act to prevent you from starting anything.

As we do less and less we realise that by doing nothing we achieve nothing and enjoy nothing. We then start to wonder why we should bother to do anything anyway. So the depressive cycle continues. The less we do the more onerous and daunting tasks appear to become and the more we procrastinate or avoid them.

7 SKILLS TO REDUCE EMOTIONAL AND COGNITIVE EFFECTS OF AROUSAL

DISTRACTION TECHNIQUES

After the accident you may find that you experience unpleasant, repetitive, intrusive thoughts that can be very distressing. One way of controlling this is through various types of distraction activities. Distraction can be used as a way of reducing the effect of repetitive, intrusive, negative thoughts or unpleasant images. Intrusive thoughts take the form of visual images that are sparked by sights, sounds, smells or tactile reminders that bring the repressed images to our awareness. Distraction techniques are particularly effective if the person is troubled by unnecessary worry.

Excessive worry about events that are unlikely to happen will only make you feel worse; it may even increase your chances of having something go wrong or of making you feel that you cannot cope.

These strategies are very practical and work well when used properly. However, you will need to experiment with them to find out which ones work best for you. Many people who try these techniques find it difficult to apply them, particularly if they are not used to dealing with their emotions in such detail. If you feel that you are also finding it hard to use them, this does not mean that you have failed or that they do not work. It may be useful to consult a health professional who can show you how to apply these and help determine which are the most appropriate for you.

These techniques include:

- **focusing on an object**
- **mental tasks**
- **increasing awareness of the environment**
- **engage in some form of physical activity**
- **pleasant imagery**
- **thought-stopping technique**
- **rubber band technique.**

It is impor-
tant however,
to keep in
mind that dis-
traction should
not be used to
deny or avoid
dealing with
painful issues.
Part of your
recovery
will involve
dealing with
painful
thoughts and
memories so
that they are
properly
processed and
put into
perspective.

Focusing on an object

Direct your attention to an object. Try to visualise it as clearly as possible. Describe it in as much detail as you can noting its size, colour, texture and position. For example, ask yourself:

'Where is it located? How large is it?'

'What could someone use it for?'

'How many different uses for it can I think of?'

Mental tasks

Try counting by multiples of three or thinking about words starting with the letter L. Absorb yourself with crosswords or puzzles, or reading a magazine or book may be another approach. It is often useful to carry a book or magazine with you and when you attend appointments in case you need to wait for any period of time.

Increasing awareness of the environment

Distract yourself by increasing your awareness of your immediate surroundings. Observe the behaviour of people around you, what they are doing, what they look like; or notice the colours, smells or movement of objects near you.

Rather than remaining by yourself in one spot, move to a window or sit out in the garden and observe the activities going on around you. Attend to the touch, taste, smell, sound and feeling of the world. This is also a good technique to use if you are caught in traffic or delayed for some other reason.

David G

Five months ago David was involved in a car accident. He was driving his seven-year-old son to his Saturday soccer match and was side-swiped by an oncoming car. No-one was injured but his son was a little shaken. The other driver was very apologetic and explained that he thought a spider was crawling up his leg and he was startled by it.

David's car received considerable damage and he was very distressed about it because he had only just bought it and it was brand new. He became very anxious about driving it and would constantly be looking at cars in the lanes next to him or behind him, watching whether they were coming too close. He would get very irritable when in the car and did not enjoy driving as much as before.

The psychologist he contacted at his local community centre suggested he try some distraction techniques, such as listening to the radio or talking to his passenger whilst driving, and when stopped in traffic or at lights to notice the scenery and buildings rather than focus attention on other drivers. With time he found that he did not feel so anxious about being in the car or about what other cars around him were doing.

Engage in some form of physical activity

Do some exercise, wash the car, take the dog for a walk, do some gardening, meet a friend for lunch.

Pleasant imagery

In depression a person is preoccupied with negative thoughts, imagery and endless worry.

Try to reverse this by actively concentrating on pleasant memories or enjoyable events.

Recall previous pleasant experiences such as an enjoyable holiday, or fantasise about what you would do if you won the lottery or were to travel the world.

Thought-stopping technique

Whenever negative or troublesome thoughts enter your mind, say 'stop' aloud at first then silently to yourself. Imagine a STOP sign and think of something else, for example, a pleasant scene. As you do this make a time with yourself to watch a 'mental video' of the trauma for 20 minutes later that day. When you have successfully stopped that negative or troublesome thought reward yourself for the effort.

Rubber band technique

Sometimes upsetting negative thoughts seem to come unpredictably. These intrusive thoughts may increase feelings of guilt and depression. They may be triggered off by events in the environment which 'remind' us of negative memories. One way of eliminating these intrusive ruminative thoughts is by the rubber band technique. Wear a rubber band loosely around the wrist. When negative thoughts enter your mind, stretch the rubber band out and let it snap back onto your wrist. Often the short, sharp sensation of pain will be sufficient to redirect your attention away from the depressing negative thought. As you do this make a time with yourself to watch a 'mental video' of the trauma for 20 minutes later that day.

Couple this technique with the pleasant imagery. After you have distracted yourself by using the rubber band switch your thoughts to pleasant images.

The last two strategies may seem silly. However, they allow you to control the intrusions rather than them seeming to control you and your time. You are setting the agenda.

All the distraction techniques described above are designed to help control and minimise unwanted, intrusive and repetitive negative thoughts that make you feel guilty or depressed. These techniques will be more effective if you use relaxation and breathing control as well. By minimising these thoughts you can begin to focus more clearly on your approach to dealing with difficulties and to regain a more positive outlook towards yourself and your environment.

THINKING STRAIGHT

If you have experienced a stress reaction you may find that you have also started thinking badly of yourself. This may be for a variety of reasons:

1 **You may think that you should have acted differently during the trauma.**

2 **You may think you are to blame for what happened or feel guilty because you survived when others may have died.**

3 **You may believe that you deserve what has happened to you.**

4 **You may think poorly of yourself because you have stress symptoms, because you are now more angry, scared or drink to excess.**

These are negative and distorted thoughts which do not help recovery. A *self-guided dialogue* is one way to overcome these negative thinking patterns. This is a term used to describe:

1 **the way in which we focus on what we are saying to ourselves, and**

2 **then trying to challenge any negative thoughts, so that they may be replaced with more realistic and helpful thoughts.**

Essentially what we are aiming to do is identify and label the irrational, faulty or negative self-statements and then substitute these with rational, accurate, flexible or self-enhancing self-statements.

It is not the events that happen in our lives that cause us concern, rather, it is our thoughts, perceptions and interpretations about those events. Negative self-statements can perpetuate avoidance, so much so that what we say to ourselves in response to a particular situation determines our mood and feelings. Therefore, the consequences for us can be less stressful by changing our thoughts or belief systems about those

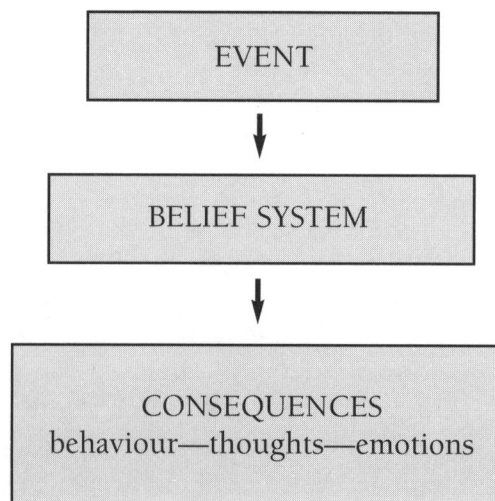

EVENT

↓

BELIEF SYSTEM

↓

CONSEQUENCES
behaviour—thoughts—emotions

events. This is because:

Another way of thinking is that our belief system is like an audio-tape in our head that has recorded upon it:

- **attitudes/beliefs from the past**
- **our biological heritage**
- **present mood and life circumstances**
- **our beliefs/thoughts about the future.**

Often our belief systems become too rigid and inflexible due to our irrational thinking. Irrational thinking is a frequent cause of stress. Thinking more rationally is an important stress management procedure.

What we need to do is to dispute these irrational ideas and beliefs with rational, flexible and positive 'self-talk' so that the outcome for our behaviour, thoughts and emotions is a positive one. For example, rather than thinking 'I should have been more careful', you might gradually believe 'I did the best I could with what I had at the time'.

Each of us has our own unique beliefs.

COPING STATEMENTS

Learning to use coping statements effectively to overcome anxiety will take practice and perseverance. The way you respond to early physical symptoms of anxiety will be determined largely by *what you say to yourself,* as illustrated below.

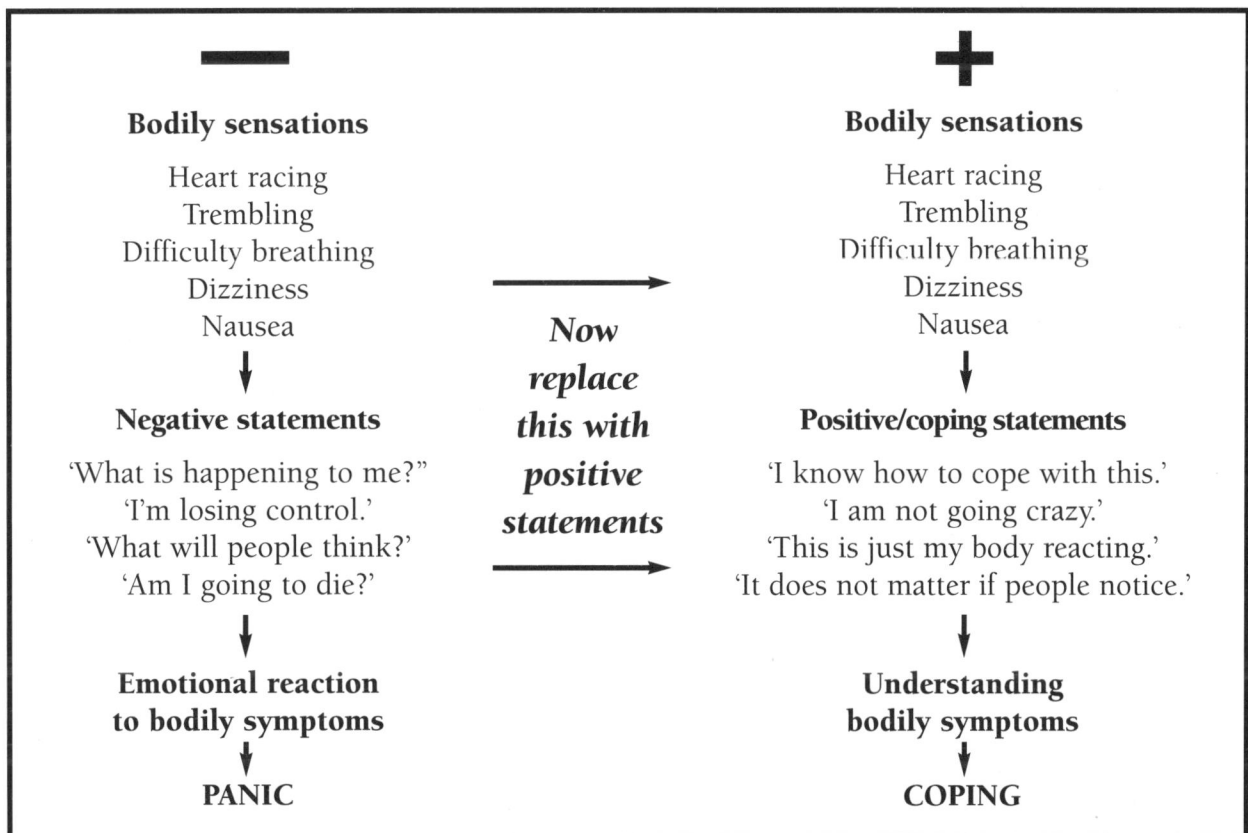

—	*Now replace this with positive statements*	+
Bodily sensations		**Bodily sensations**
Heart racing		Heart racing
Trembling		Trembling
Difficulty breathing		Difficulty breathing
Dizziness		Dizziness
Nausea		Nausea
↓		↓
Negative statements		**Positive/coping statements**
'What is happening to me?"		'I know how to cope with this.'
'I'm losing control.'		'I am not going crazy.'
'What will people think?'		'This is just my body reacting.'
'Am I going to die?'		'It does not matter if people notice.'
↓		↓
Emotional reaction to bodily symptoms		**Understanding bodily symptoms**
↓		↓
PANIC		**COPING**

Below are some other *coping statements* that you may find useful to develop your attitudes of self acceptance. If one statement gets tiresome or seems to stop being effective, try another.

'I can be anxious and still deal with this situation.'

'I can handle these symptoms and sensations.'

'This isn't the worse thing that could happen.'

'I'll ride this through, I don't need to let this get to me.'

'I deserve to feel OK right now.'

'There's no need to push myself. I can take as small a step forward as I choose.'

'I don't need these thoughts, I can choose to think differently.'

'This isn't an emergency. It's OK to think slowly about what I need to do.'

'This anxiety won't hurt me, even if it doesn't feel good.'

'Don't worry, be happy.' (Use this to inject an element of lightness or humour.)

PRACTICAL EXERCISE

Using the table below, fill the left-hand side box with your *irrational self-statements* and then dispute them with *rational self-statements* on the right-hand side. Remember, negative and unhelpful thoughts can make you anxious, unhappy and physically uncomfortable and may make it harder for you to achieve things.

Irrational self-statements	Rational self-statements
eg. What has happened shouldn't have happened. It's all my fault!	eg. I can take positive steps to prepare for possible problems. I had done the best at the time. That was all anyone could have done.

8 DEALING WITH BEHAVIOURAL REACTIONS

The way we feel emotionally and the way we think affects the way we behave. Behaviour is what other people see. The response to a severe trauma following the accident can change the way we behave, emphasise certain patterns of behaviour, or develop new ways of behaving.

The following are examples of behaviours that can result as a consequence of a trauma following the accident:

- **withdrawal from those close to you**
- **losing interest in going out socially**
- **frequent crying spells**
- **aggressive behaviour**
- **overeating or under-eating**
- **avoiding travelling in cars**
- **drinking before travelling in a car as a passenger.**

In addition to the above responses three forms of negative coping strategies need to be addressed in more detail. These are avoidance, alcohol and/or drug abuse and domestic/family violent behaviours.

AVOIDANCE

When we have experienced a traumatic event and are suffering stress reactions it is common for us to experience constant recollections of the event, to feel as if we are reliving the event and to be fearful about coming into contact with anything or any situation that reminds us of that event. These reactions lead to avoidance of the location where the event took place, and not wanting to talk or think about the event, and to emotional numbness.

Unfortunately, there is every danger that to 'outsiders' it may often look as if you have overcome the event.

Avoidance behaviour is, in effect, one of the main features of Acute Stress Disorder and Post-Traumatic Stress Disorder. After a traumatic event many things that are rationally and irrationally related to the trauma can trigger a severe sense of anxiety for us. Avoiding a situation that frightens us is, more than anything else, behaviour that will keep those fears alive. The avoidance can be of sufficient strength that we may never again enter the situation and therefore never know whether or not it would, in fact, trigger an anxiety attack. The issue, then, is one of being in control.

Those of us who are suffering from immediate stress responses come to learn which situations cause us to be anxious and out of control. The situation is not necessarily directly related to the traumatic event but through a process of generalisation the situation becomes connected to that event.

We learn that through avoidance behaviour we can control our anxiety and fear, however irrational. The more we reinforce the use of avoidance behaviour to be in control physically and cognitively, the more probable the anxiety producing situation will develop into a very strong fear or phobia.

Phobias develop because it is very rewarding to avoid facing situations that cause us anxiety. As long as we continue to avoid dealing with a phobic situation, activity or object the phobia will remain securely in place.

AVOIDANCE OF DRIVING

A minority of people involved in road trauma develop an intense phobia of driving to the extent that they experience panic whenever they contemplate driving and/or remain unable to enter a motor vehicle. The major fears include:

- **fear of another accident happening**
- **fear of being trapped inside a motor vehicle**
- **fear of being severely injured**
- **fear of travelling when others are driving.**

The phobic person may become preoccupied with thoughts of having to drive. They may make excuses in order to avoid having to go driving, or they may feel extremely anxious when faced with the prospect of actually having to go for a drive. There is a risk that the person may turn to, and become reliant on, medication or alcohol to help them to cope.

The majority of people involved in motor vehicle accidents tend to develop not a phobia in the true sense of the word but, rather, what is best described as a reluctance to drive. This means that the person does not actively avoid driving but essentially prefers not to or to limit the amount of driving he/she does. Thus:

- **Driving is restricted to the bare minimum, usually travelling to and from work.**
- **Driving is no longer enjoyable or relaxing.**
- **There is a sense of discomfort or tension when travelling in a motor vehicle.**
- **Driving as a pastime or form of recreation is no longer engaged in, for example, going for a drive to the country or to a picnic.**

Phobias and a reluctance to drive can be reduced by the use of anxiety management techniques coupled with *systematic desensitisation.*

SYSTEMATIC DESENSITISATION

This is a relaxation-based approach with a history of proven effectiveness in the treatment of phobias. The technique is a simple one that combines physical relaxation and mental images. Its aim is to reduce the level of physical arousal and anxiety experienced when a person visualises a traumatic scene or recalls an unpleasant memory.

What happens when you are confronted with a frightening situation?

Most people will become anxious and try to escape. Later, they become sensitised, that is, they are more likely to react anxiously in anticipation of coming into contact with the situation again. For example, if a pedestrian was hit at a crossing, they will be reminded of the accident every time they approach a pedestrian crossing, when watching someone cross a road during a television program or even looking at the cover of the Beatles album which shows the foursome crossing Abbey Road. Martha, a 52-year-old married housewife, was struck by a motorcyclist while walking across the road near her home. She was on her way to visit her neighbour for their usual weekly tea and chat. On discharge from hospital she found herself becoming extremely panicky every time she headed off towards her neighbour's house. She began to avoid the situation by walking in the opposite direction, and crossing a block further down where there was a set of lights. She then walked around the block just to avoid passing the section of the road where she was injured.

The more she did this, the stronger her fear grew, to the point where she became highly anxious even walking out of her front door. She could not bear the thought of looking at the accident scene because it acted as a reminder.

How could she overcome this problem? Well, by learning a procedure which involved gradually exposing herself to the feared situation while remaining relaxed, she eventually regained her confidence and ability to cross the road closer and closer to where the accident happened. This procedure is called systematic desensitisation and is the treatment of choice in overcoming phobic avoidance.

Systematic desensitisation may be carried out by imagining the situation or it can be practised in real life. Some people find it too difficult to confront the situation in real life. The best approach under these circumstances is to relax and visualise the scene. Once this has effectively reduced your anxiety, you will be able to apply the same principles in real life. That is, you will relax and then gradually approach easy situations and remain there until you feel comfortable and your anxiety has reduced to nothing. The next step is to pick increasingly more difficult situations and repeat the procedure until all anxiety has gone.

This procedure is difficult to do on your own, and if not done properly may lead to some worsening of your anxiety condition. Therefore it is highly recommended that you seek professional help and guidance in learning this technique. A clinical psychologist or mental health counsellor who has been trained in this technique can help you learn the skills quickly.

Having said that, it is perhaps useful to give you a basic understanding of the steps involved. If the anxiety associated with some situations is relatively minor, that is, it causes only mild discomfort, you may wish to try the technique first, either on your own or under the supervision of your partner.

If you choose to try on your own, remember that if you are having problems, you should immediately consult your local doctor, health professional counsellor or community health centre for further advice and guidance.

There are two major parts to the procedure. First, you must learn a simple muscle relaxation technique, and second, write down a hierarchy of anxious situations. By hierarchy we mean a list of situations which vary in anxiety, starting from the least anxiety-provoking to the most distressing situation that you fear.

Let us now outline the procedure which involves the following steps:

- **Learn a simple muscle relaxation technique. Relaxation techniques that may be used are described in Chapter Four of this book or may be available commercially on tapes. These tapes are often on sale through bookshops or community centres.**

- **Now you need to construct a hierarchy of scenes of increasing anxiety associated with the traumatic event. Rate each scene on a scale of 0–100, where zero means no anxiety and 100 means maximum anxiety. To do this think of all the situations that you avoid because they remind you of the trauma. List these and then read through them to decide which situation causes you the least amount of stress. Give this a rating of 1. Do the same with the next scene that would cause you the next level of least anxiety and rate this with the number 2. Work through the rest of the situations on the list so that the ones which cause you the most distress are given higher ratings.**

An example of what Martha's list may look like is shown below.

Situation/Scene	Rank/Order	Subjective units of distress (SUDS rating, 0–100)
Crossing the road where the accident occurred	10	100
Walking to the scene of the accident but not crossing the road	9	91
Crossing the road within 2 metres of the accident scene	8	83
Walking to the scene with her pet dog	7	76
Crossing at nearby pedestrian crossing	6	67
Walking around the block to friend's house	5	55
Walking towards road where accident happened	4	49
Walking onto footpath along road outside her house	3	34
Walking around in her front yard	2	21
Stepping out of her front door	1	10

You are now ready to apply the technique in imagination. Here are the steps to take.

- **Select a quiet environment, make yourself comfortable and begin the muscle relaxation.**
- **When sufficiently relaxed, begin to think of the least anxious scene in the hierarchy.**
- **Continue relaxing with the image.**
- **If the image causes anxiety, continue relaxing with that image until the anxiety reduces in strength. You may need to stop thinking of the image, to focus on the relaxation and then once relaxed, recall the image.**
- **Once you are able to visualise a scene with minimal anxiety proceed to the next scene in the hierarchy that you have constructed.**

Always ensure that the strength of the anxiety associated with the image is less at the end of the session than at the beginning. *Never* give up as the anxiety is increasing as this will act to further sensitise the anxiety associated with that scene. *Always* end the session on a note of decreasing anxiety.

Once you are comfortable with imagining the anxiety-provoking situation, you may wish to apply the systematic desensitisation in real life. To do this, return to your hierarchy of anxious situations. Take the situation which is least anxiety-provoking. Spend several minutes relaxing using your tape or muscle relaxation instructions. Then gradually approach the anxiety-provoking situation, continuing to focus on the relaxation as you do so. If the anxiety rises too quickly, do not walk away. Rather, you need to stay there and continue relaxing until such time as the anxiety starts to reduce to low levels. Once the anxiety has reduced, you may choose to continue or stay there relaxing further. When you feel comfortable, you may then walk away from the scene. Do not walk away from the situation if your anxiety is high and rising. This will only serve to aggravate your avoidance behaviour. You must stay in the situation until the anxiety goes. This is one reason why you must exercise caution in doing this procedure on your own. It is best to start under the supervision of a skilled professional who can monitor and support your progress through each step.

Kelly F

Kelly, a 25-year-old married housewife, was a front-seat passenger in a motor vehicle that was involved in a side impact collision at a busy intersection. She remembers her car slowly proceeding across the intersection when she looked to her left to see a van approaching rapidly. She realised that the van was travelling too fast to avoid a collision. On impact, her vehicle spun before coming to rest on the wrong side of the road. She was trapped for 15 minutes. Her injuries included fractures to both ankles, lacerations to her legs, face and arms, and bruising to her chest.

Although she recovered well physically, she suffered restricted head movement and persistent mild headaches. She reported that she was unable to be a passenger in a motor vehicle. She refused to travel but, when forced to, would consume several glasses of alcohol before lying in the back seat of the car with her head under a blanket.

Her intense phobia persisted for several months until she was treated by systematic desensitisation. Following eight sessions over three months her anxiety reduced markedly to the point where she was able to travel as a rear seat passenger without the aid of alcohol.

ALCOHOL AND/OR DRUG ABUSE

Alcohol or drug abuse is another common coping method used by people who have suffered from severe trauma. Primarily, alcohol and/or drugs can be used to dull our mind to traumatic memories, or to block feelings of shame and guilt. At first this will appear to be an easy solution. However, our body soon becomes used to the alcohol or drugs. As the tolerance level of the body increases, more and more alcohol is needed to have the same effect of dulling the memories and the feelings associated with them. In time the body becomes dependent on the drug so that if we try to do without it we will suffer severe withdrawal symptoms.

It is important to note that, initially, alcohol acts as a stimulant; however, within a few hours of drinking, it begins to act as a depressant. The side-effects of alcohol or drug abuse are numerous. It can cause an inability to function appropriately at work, as well as cause us to be socially withdrawn or to behave inappropriately. It is also important to note that driving under the influence is not only dangerous but it is also illegal.

When trying to stop or reduce the intake of alcohol or drugs, it is advised that you consult your doctor or local drug and alcohol counsellor. You might require help for withdrawal symptoms.

Patrick S

Patrick, a 32-year-old mechanic, was riding his motorcycle home from work one afternoon when a car pulled out of a driveway in front of him. Unable to stop, Patrick managed to swerve out of the way but lost control and hit a nearby power pole. He suffered a broken leg and a fractured pelvis. As a result the doctors told him that he would be unable to return to work for at least eight months. He became increasingly irritable, experienced outbursts of anger and had severe depression. He refused to take medication as prescribed by his doctor and turned to marijuana to numb the pain. He began to drink heavily and became completely isolated and withdrawn.

One afternoon his flatmate found him unconscious on the lounge room floor. When they rushed him to the local Emergency Department they found he had tried to kill himself by taking an overdose of pills.

DOMESTIC/FAMILY VIOLENCE

Domestic violence and/or family violence could be a symptom of Post-Traumatic Stress Disorder or it could cause a traumatic reaction. The person who is being violent could have been exposed to a severely traumatic event. The violence could be considered a manifestation of the feelings of anger and depression as a result of the original trauma.

This does not, however, excuse that person for any violent behaviour.

Everyone has a right to feel safe and to live without violence.

It is important to be aware of the danger of this happening to you and to seek assistance if you find yourself in this situation.

MEMORIES AND INTRUSIVE THOUGHTS

Memories and intrusive thoughts about a traumatic event can shape a person's behaviour, actions and emotional reactions. Many of the features of a post-trauma reaction are also directly or indirectly linked in some way to the recollection of unpleasant memories.

As mentioned earlier, painful and distressing images repeatedly intrude into a person's consciousness. The person responds by attempting to force these thoughts or images out only to find that they continually recur. As a result, the person becomes more anxious, agitated, irritable and aroused, and too preoccupied with the anticipation that such images will continue to occur and eventually may overwhelm them, sending them 'insane'.

Paradoxically, the more you attempt to resist traumatic images the more they become reinforced and consolidated. Why is this the case? Let us demonstrate by giving an example of the processes involved:

1   **Think of the number '5'.**

2   **Now put it out of your mind completely.**

3   **Wait ten minutes and then see if you can recall what the number was.**

It is guaranteed that you will be unable to forget the number. Why? Because every time you attempt to forget the number, you say to yourself subconsciously, 'Forget the number. What number should I forget? The number 5!' This has the effect of reminding you of the number and forcing you to keep remembering it.

So too with unpleasant images. Every time you try to force out a traumatic image, you are asking yourself 'What image should I forget? The image of...[the trauma]...'.

Again, at odd times the thought may enter your mind, 'I hope the image does not recur. What image?... the image of the trauma!' and so on.

This process is all the more powerful in traumatic stress reactions because of the strong emotions attached to the distressing images. However, it is important to remember that these thoughts are only memories and that with time you will learn not to feel so distressed by them. Practising the relaxation techniques that you have learnt in this book can help to reduce the distress and discomfort these memories can cause. If you find that these thoughts and memories are particularly persistent and disturbing it is advisable to seek professional assistance as soon as possible.

PRACTICAL EXERCISE To obtain maximum benefit from treatment and to help monitor progress over time, it is necessary to have a clear idea in mind of the specific goals and objectives you want to achieve. It is important, therefore, to take some time to clarify clearly and concisely the nature of the problems and difficulties you are experiencing, and the manner in which they are interfering with your well-being.

First, we want you to list the psychological symptoms you are suffering at present, for example, 'I get panicky if I have to get into a car'; 'I feel very low and depressed'; 'I startle easily'. Try to arrange these in decreasing order of severity or importance.

Symptoms

Now try to list in what ways or in what area of day to day functioning these symptoms cause difficulties and/or interfere with your quality of life. For example, anxiety prevents me going out; irritability causes me to be cranky with others; I feel low and want to be by myself.

Impact of symptoms on daily living
Now write down the sort of changes you would like to see happen, for example, spending more time socialising, being less cranky, feeling more relaxed and less jumpy.

Desired changes

To measure changes over time, it is useful to record the frequency and intensity of symptoms as they occur. To do this you need to write the symptom down when it happens or make a mental note of it if you are unable to jot it down. However, relying on your memory may not be as effective as writing it down. It is recommended that you record the following:

Time	Date	Symptoms	What triggered the symptom	Intensity on a 10 point scale	How long it lasted

Another behavioural problem that may arise is 'disturbed' sleep. Let's look more closely at the topic of sleep disturbance, including the recurrent dreams, as they are highly distressing to those suffering from traumatic stress reactions.

SLEEP DISTURBANCE

After your accident you may find that your sleep pattern changes. You may find that you have problems getting to sleep, do not have a restful sleep and/or are constantly awakened by vivid dreams. As a result you may feel tired, find it difficult to concentrate and feel detached from others.

If you have these symptoms just keep in mind that what you are experiencing is normal, it is just a way for your body to tell you that it is recuperating from a traumatic event. Dreaming is essential for mental and physical well-being.

Other factors and causes that may contribute to your inability to obtain an adequate quality and quantity of sleep include:[9]

- **anxiety**
- **unexpressed anger or resentment over your predicament**
- **disorders of mood, eg. depression**
- **sleeping or napping excessively during the day, etc.**

Deprivation of REM (Rapid Eye Movement), or dream sleep, also has a negative effect on your sense of well-being, leading to:

- **increased irritability**
- **increased anxiety or tension during the waking hours.**

You also need to be aware of the effects of medication on dreaming and sleep. Some medications interfere with dreaming. When medication is stopped there is a rebound effect where the number of dreams and their vividness increases dramatically. Be aware that this is a temporary reaction and will stop after a few nights. Try to tolerate these dreams knowing that they will cease very soon.

Be aware that long-term use of medication may be more harmful. This is because medication can cause further depression of the nervous system and this chemical depression only aggravates insomnia and psychological symptoms.

To improve the quality of your sleep you need to:[10]

- **Go to bed only when you are sleepy.**
- **Use the bed and the bedroom only for sleep and sex (ie. no reading, watching television, eating, or working during the day or at night).**
- **Get out of bed and go into another room whenever you are unable to sleep for 15–20 minutes, and return only when sleepy again.**
- **Go to bed at the same time every night and arise at the same time every morning. An occasional sleepless night does very little harm.**
- **Avoid taking a nap during the day.**

Here are further useful techniques that may help you sleep:

- **Exercising in the morning or afternoon is an excellent way of producing a state of pleasant fatigue which helps induce a good night's sleep. However, you should not exercise late in the evening or just before going to bed. This is because the immediate effect of exercise is to stimulate the system.**

- **Waking in the middle of the night is sometimes a problem and it is better to get up and read a book than to lie in bed tossing and turning. Eating, drinking, smoking and television are bad if you wake in the middle of the night. The best advice is simply to read a book or do some very light stretches to relax the muscles.**

- **Use relaxation techniques before sleep and if woken during the night.**

- **Hot baths can be very relaxing and are useful just before going to bed.**

- **Over-stimulation from loud noises, including music, is not a good thing late at night. However, soft, soothing and relaxing music can help you go to sleep.**

One basic rule is not to worry about how much sleep you get as this will only create further stress.

USE OF MEDICATION IN POST TRAUMA

Medication may be a useful additional tool in helping people cope with symptoms of anxiety or depression but it should not be used as the only treatment strategy.

Medication can be used when:

- **symptoms are so intense that they prevent you using adaptive coping skills, for example, intense anxiety and physical arousal, depression or sleep disturbance**

- **if you suffer symptoms of excessive physical arousal such as panicky feelings, being easily startled, or a racing heart.**

Medication is not generally useful in overcoming avoidance behaviours, feelings of numbness or sense of vulnerability unless these symptoms are the result of the presence of depression.

The most typical medications used for the following symptoms are:

Anxiety and excessive physical arousal
Anti-anxiety drugs:
Benzodiazepines (Valium, Ducene, Xanax, Ativan)
Buspirone (Buspar)
Beta Blockers (Propanalol)
Clonidine

Sleep disturbance
Benzodiazepines (especially short acting such as Valium)
Tricyclics (Amitriptyline, Doxepin).

Depression
Antidepressants :
Tricyclic antidepressants (Tryptanol)
Monoamine oxidase inhibitors (Parnate)
Serotonin reuptake inhibitors (Zoloft, Prozac).

A number of issues need to be considered when using drugs. Some medications, such as the benzodiazepines, need to be used with caution where there is evidence of aggressive behaviour. Valium may have a disinhibitory effect that may weaken a person's control over violent or aggressive outbursts.

Also, there is a danger that people may attribute any positive change in symptoms simply to the medication rather than to any other part of the treatment that they receive. As a result, there is a risk of a relapse in symptoms when the medication is stopped. The fear that symptoms will return if medication ceases leads to people becoming psychologically dependant upon such medication.

Remember

Improvement is often due to changes in behaviour, cognitions and non-medication treatment strategies designed to reduce arousal; it is not only because of medication.

With some medications there is a possibility that some anxiety symptoms may re-emerge. This anxiety is part of the withdrawal process from that medication. *It is not a signal that the original anxiety symptoms are returning.* In most cases these symptoms disappear within a week or two.

Recurring nightmares and bad dreams are a distressing part of post-trauma reactions. Be aware that the effect of some medications is to suppress what is known as REM sleep.

REM sleep, or Rapid Eye Movement sleep, is that period of sleep during which dreams occur. When medication is stopped there is an increase in the REM activity, a feature that is called REM-rebound. It is almost as if the body were catching up on lost dream time. This rebound usually lasts two to five nights and is characterised by a period of frequent and vivid dreaming. Again, it is a temporary process and the dreams are different from, and unrelated to, the nightmares experienced in post-trauma reactions.

9 WAYS OF COPING WITH RELAPSE

Over the last few chapters we looked at ways of coping with stress and anxiety through a variety of techniques. Sometimes, despite the practice of these techniques, you may feel as if you are slipping backwards or relapsing. This section therefore looks at ways of preventing relapse and how to cope with it if it occurs.

RELAPSE AND RELAPSE PREVENTION

Relapse is a feeling that you are going backwards in your treatment program. A relapse is often viewed as devastating because it has a lot of emotional meaning for the person who has put considerable effort into recovering. However, what it may be indicating is that you are attempting too much too soon. Therefore, it is important not to resign yourself to getting worse but to actively take charge of the relapse and overcome it. It is also important to realise that relapses are expected at the time of anniversaries (eg. of the accident, birthdays, special holidays), and that the few days before are likely to be the worst. Try to remember that this is only temporary and focus on the progress that you have made up to this time.

While you feel stressed do not ignore what you have learnt through this book, but try to maintain the gains you have already made. *Remember that ups and downs in the recovery process are the rule rather than the exception.*

There are many things you can do to prevent relapse. These may include maintaining good physical health by getting adequate nutrition and exercise, and by limiting your intake of stimulants such as tea, coffee and smoking cigarettes. Prolonged use of alcohol is also detrimental to health and can make you more susceptible to physical and/or psychological illness.

Prepare your body and your mind for those stressful situations. Use the techniques you have learnt to help you cope with anxiety and stress. If you do not feel ready for a particular event do not force yourself to do it unless you really want to. Do not participate in activities that leave you mentally drained for the sake of pleasing other people.

Keep practising your relaxation exercises and breath control skills even when you do not feel especially anxious. These techniques take time to master and lack of practice can result in some loss of skills. You will be less likely to control your anxiety if those skills are rusty.

Finally, use the positive thinking exercises to maintain a positive

When you cope with the relapses effectively, your progress to recovery will still continue. A positive attitude means taking charge of your anxiety rather than letting it take charge of you.

frame of mind. Poor self-esteem and lack of confidence are directly related to negative self-statements that can be changed. Remember to always reward yourself for coping with your anxiety symptoms.

Acknowledge your successes!

Therefore, if you have a relapse do not add to the problem with all the old catastrophic, emotional and self-destructive ideas, such as:

'What is happening to me?'
'Am I falling apart?'
'Are my symptoms worsening again?'

Remember to keep practising all the techniques you have been reading about and you will make progress.

HELPFUL EVERYDAY TECHNIQUES
Here is a summary of a few helpful everyday techniques you may like to use to lessen your anxiety and stress, and thus reduce the chance of a relapse occurring.

PHYSICAL
1 **Get plenty of rest, even if you cannot sleep.**
2 **Try to eat regular and well-balanced meals.**
3 **Regular exercise (eg. walking, cycling or jogging) is good for reducing the physical effects of stress and trauma.**
4 **Reduce your stimulant intake such as tea, coffee, chocolate, cola and cigarettes. Your body is already 'hyped up' and these substances only increase your level of arousal.**
5 **Do not try to numb the pain with drugs or alcohol; this will lead to more problems in the long term.**
6 **Make time for relaxation. Learn techniques such as progressive muscle relaxation, breathing exercises, or even meditation or yoga.**

EMOTIONAL
1 **Give yourself permission to 'feel rotten' or 'lousy'—you have been through a traumatic experience.**
2 **Feeling bad is unpleasant but do not overreact—you can cope with it for a while.**

THOUGHTS

1 Recurring thoughts, dreams and flashbacks are normal. Do not try to fight them. They will decrease and become less painful in time.

2 Talk about the incident, your reactions and how you are feeling to people who care about you. Even though this process is painful it is the best way of coming to terms with your experiences.

3 You might find that keeping a journal or a diary is very helpful. When you cannot talk to others about how you feel writing it down is almost as good.

BEHAVIOUR

1 Try to resume a normal routine as quickly as possible, but remember to take it easy; do not throw yourself into activities or work in an attempt to avoid the unpleasant feelings and memories.

2 Sometimes you will want to be alone, however, try not to become too isolated. Contact friends and, if necessary, have someone stay with you for a few hours each day.

3 Do things you enjoy and be nice to yourself. Try to schedule at least one pleasurable activity each day.

4 You may wish to try to help others who have been through similar situations; your support and understanding may be very important to them.

5 Do not make any major life decisions (such as moving house or changing jobs) in the period following the trauma. However, do make as many smaller, daily decisions as possible (eg. what you want to eat or what film you would like to see). This will help you to re-establish a feeling of control over your life.

FINAL NOTE

Please remember that this self-help guide is aimed at helping you to understand the types of reactions that are commonly experienced after road trauma. It is also aimed at describing the types of techniques that can be helpful in dealing with these reactions. This book is best used in conjunction with professional treatment, and is not a substitute for therapy.

Many people who experience the types of reactions we have discussed in this book feel that they should be able to cope on their own and they feel ashamed to ask for help. They try to cope by avoiding people, places and activities that remind them of the trauma and their situation. They become socially isolated and withdrawn and often turn to drugs and alcohol to help numb the pain.

We acknowledge that it is difficult to ask for help, especially when the symptoms have been around for a long time. But we cannot stress enough the importance of seeking help for these types of reactions. There are many health professionals who have been trained to deal specifically with post-traumatic stress reactions, and who are sensitive, supportive and very understanding of these problems. You do not need to feel ashamed or weak at asking for help. You have a right to seek help if you need it.

Please contact your local general practitioner, community health centre or relevant professional organisation today and take that vital first step.

BE PROUD OF
YOUR ACHIEVEMENTS

APPENDIX
Relevant organisations

ANXIETY DISORDERS FOUNDATION OF AUSTRALIA (NSW BRANCH) INC

PO Box 6198
Shopping World
North Sydney NSW 2060
Phone: 016 282 897
Fax: (02) 9716 0416

AUSTRALASIAN SOCIETY FOR TRAUMATIC STRESS STUDIES INC

PO Box 4048
Richmond East VIC 3121
Phone/Fax: (03) 9421 0326

BANKSTOWN CLINIC FOR ANXIETY AND TRAUMATIC STRESS

Bankstown Hospital
Claribel Street, Bankstown NSW 2200
Phone: (02) 9722 8992
Fax: (02) 9722 8964

CLINIC FOR ANXIETY AND TRAUMATIC STRESS

Psychiatry Research and Teaching Unit
Health Services Building
Liverpool Hospital NSW 2170
Phone: (02) 9828 4902
Fax: (02) 9828 4910

CLINICAL RESEARCH UNIT FOR ANXIETY DISORDERS (CRUFAD)

St Vincents Hospital
299 Forbes Street
Darlinghurst NSW 2010
Phone: (02) 9332 1013
Fax: (02) 9332 4316

COMMUNITY HEALTH CENTRES
(please consult your local white pages for the centre nearest to you)

MENTAL HEALTH ASSOCIATION (NSW)

62 Victoria Road
Gladesville NSW 2111
Phone: (02) 9816 1611

NATIONAL ASSOCIATION FOR LOSS AND GRIEF (NSW) INC

PO Box 79
Turramurra NSW 2074
Phone: (02) 9988 3376
Fax: (02) 9988 3856

POST-TRAUMATIC STRESS DISORDER UNIT

Department of Medical Psychology
Westmead Hospital
Westmead NSW 2145
Phone: (02) 9845 7979

ROAD TRAUMA SUPPORT TEAM INC

ACT Region

Grant Cameron Community Centre
27 Mulley Street
Holder ACT 2611
Phone: (02) 6287 4266

Northern Tasmania

PO Box 1963
Launceston TAS 7250
Phone: (03) 6334 9010

TRAUMA CARE PTY LTD

48 Amphitheatre Circuit
Baulkham Hills NSW 2153
Phone: (02) 9838 9001

POST-TRAUMATIC STRESS DISORDER PROGRAM (NON-WAR TRAUMA)

Wesley Private Hospital
91 Milton Street
Ashfield NSW 2131
Phone: (02) 9797 7133

FURTHER READING

Allen, J.G., *Coping with Trauma: A Guide to Self-Understanding,* American Psychiatric Press, Washington, 1995.

Blanchard, E.B. & Hickling, E.J., *After the Crash. Assessment and Treatment of Motor Vehicle Accident Survivors,* American Psychological Association, Washington, 1997.

Marks, I., *Living with Fear,* McGraw-Hill, New York, 1978.

Mitchell, M., *The Aftermath of Road Accidents. Psychological, Social and Legal Consequences of an Everyday Trauma,* Routledge, London, 1997.

Peterson, K.C., Prout, M.F. & Schwarz, R.A., *Post-Traumatic Stress Disorder. A Clinician's Guide,* Plenum Press, New York, 1991.

Silove, D. & Manicavasagar, V., *Overcoming Panic,* Robinson, London, 1997.

Tanner, S. & Ball, J., *Beating the Blues,* Doubleday, Sydney, 1989.

Trickett, S., *Coping with Anxiety and Depression,* Sheldon Press, London, 1989.

van der Kolk, B.A., McFarlane, A.C. & Weisaeth, L., *Traumatic Stress. The Effects of Overwhelming Experience on Mind, Body and Society,* The Guildford Press, New York, 1996.

Watts, R. & de L. Horne, D.J., *Coping with Trauma. The Victim and the Helper,* Australian Academic Press, Brisbane, 1994.

ENDNOTES

1   Federal Office of Road Safety (1997), *Road Fatalities Australia,* 1996 statistical summary. Federal Office of Road Safety, Commonwealth of Australia.

2   Malt, U. (1988), The long-term psychiatric consequences of accidental injury: A longitudinal study of 107 adults, *British Journal of Psychiatry,* 153, 810–18.

3   Kuch, K., Swinson, R.P. & Kirby, M. (1985), Post-traumatic stress disorder after car accidents, *Canadian Journal of Psychiatry,* 30, 426–27.

4   Hickling, E.J. & Blanchard, E.B. (1992), Post-traumatic stress disorder and motor vehicle accidents, *Journal of Anxiety Disorders,* 6, 285–91.

5   Worden, W. (1995), *Grief Counselling, Grief Therapy,* Tavistock Publications, London.

6   Andrews, G., Crino, R., Hunt, C., Lampe, L. & Page, A. (1994), *The Treatment of Anxiety Disorders, Clinician's Guide and Patient Manuals,* Cambridge University Press, New York.

7   Matruglio, T. (1994), *Plaintiffs and the Process of Litigation,* Civil Justice Research Centre, The Law Foundation of New South Wales.

8   Goldstein, A.P. & Keller, H. (1987), *Aggressive Behaviour: Assessment and Intervention,* Pergamon Press, New York.

9   Brightthope, I. & Fitzgerald, P. (1990), *You Can Sleep Soundly Every Night Without Drugs: A Proven Self-Help Program,* Bay Books, Sydney.

10   Morin, C.M., Culbert, J.P. & Schwartz, S.M. (1994), Non-pharmocological interventions for insomnia: A meta-analysis of treatment efficacy, *American Journal of Psychiatry,* 151, 1172–80.

INDEX